HAUNTED MISSISSIPPI DELTA AND BEYOND

Other Pelican Titles by Barbara Sillery

The Haunting of Cape Cod and the Islands
Haunted Cape Cod
Haunted Cape Cod's Sea Captains, Shipwrecks, and Spirits
The Haunting of Louisiana
Haunted Louisiana
The Haunting of Mississippi

HAUNTED MISSISSIPPI DELTA AND BEYOND

BARBARA SILLERY

Haunted America

PELICAN PUBLISHING
New Orleans

The word "Pelican" and the depiction of a pelican are trademarks of Arcadia Publishing Company Inc. and are registered in the U.S. Patent and Trademark Office.

ISBN 9781455626946
Ebook ISBN 9781455626953

All photographs by Barbara Sillery

Printed in the United States of America
Published by Pelican Publishing
New Orleans, LA
www.pelicanpub.com

To my newest muses:
Michael Timothy Moore
Leila Sillery Moore

Contents

Stories and tall tales often stir up a few quirky characters.

Prologue

Take a stand, take a stand, take a stand
If I never, never see you any more
Take a stand, take a stand, take a stand
I'll meet you on that other shore.
—Charley Patton, "Prayer of Death"

The Mississippi Delta is a land of converging cultures, rocked in the cradle of its often moody, brooding, bawdy, blues music. Emotions are raw, ragged, and deeply powerful. Musicians and storytellers lay bare their souls. Myths, legends, and fear of the unknown fuel imaginations. Captured in lyrics, everyday trials and victories, large and small, enabled the inhabitants of the Delta region to endure, to express their feelings, to thrive, and to celebrate a shared heritage. Beyond the Delta, from Tupelo to Columbus, from the state's capital to Oxford, Mississippi stories and tall tales are passed from generation to generation.

Ghost stories are a crossover genre, venturing into the fields of anthropology, biography, geography, philosophy, religion, and sociology. Phantoms lurk behind every door and slip along pathways.

I am grateful to so many flesh-and-bone Mississippians for opening their doors and sharing family histories, legends, and personal encounters with their favorite spirits. Many, many, thanks to: Marsha Colson, Mattie Jo Ratcliffe, Gay Guerico, Lynn Bradford, Carolyn Guido, Margaret Guido, Jeanette Feltus, Cheryl Morace, Elizabeth Boggess, Katherine Blankenstein, Patricia Taylor, Kay McNeil, Judy Grimsley, Thomas Miller, Eric Williams, Chris Brinkley, Tom Pharr, Phyllis Small, John

Kellogg, Joe Connor, Kathy Hall, Leonard Fuller, Bob Mazelle, Leyland French, Nancy Carpenter, Dixie Butler, Grayce Hicks, Leigh Imes, Melanie Snow, James Denning, Donna White, Richard Forte, Al Allen, David Gautier, Aimée Gautier Dugger, Mark Wallace, Wesley Smith, Lisa Winters, John Puddin' Moore, Dominick Cross, Warren Harper, Mike Jones, Woody Wilkins, Clay Williams, Ruth Cole, Lucy Allen, William Griffith, Drew Chiles, Dick Guyton, Sybil Presley Clark, Lisa Hall, Tracie Maxey-Conwill, and Tom Booth.

To Pat Dottore, thank you for catching my run-on sentences; every writer should have a former English teacher and school supervisor in their corner. To the staff at Pelican Publishing, especially Editor in Chief Nina Kooij, you have been terrific to work with.

To my daughters Heather Bell Genter and Rebecca Genter, who bring me joy and urge me on, I wouldn't make it through anything without you. An extra-special thank-you to my eldest daughter, Danielle Genter Moore, who patiently pored over the chapters and tried to keep me on track. Her on-target corrections and notes always elicited a smile, a few groans, and occasional chuckles.

To the lively and intriguing spirits of Mississippi, it's been a pleasure. "I'll meet you on that other shore."

Lagniappe: Each of the chapters ends with *lagniappe* (lan yap), a Creole term for a little something extra. When a customer makes a purchase, the merchant often includes a small gift. The tradition dates back to the seventeenth century in France. When weighing the grain, the shop keeper would add a few extra kernels *pour la nappe* (for the cloth), as some of the grains tended to stick to the fibers of the material. In New Orleans, where I lived for more than three decades, lagniappe is an accepted daily practice. It is a form of good will, like the thirteenth rose in a bouquet of a dozen long-stemmed roses. The lagniappe at the end of each chapter offers additional background on the ghost or haunted site—perhaps just enough more to entice you to visit the Mississippi Delta region and beyond and seek your own conclusions.

HAUNTED MISSISSIPPI DELTA AND BEYOND

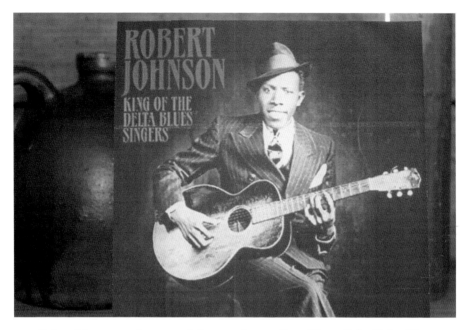

Robert Johnson on the cover of the compilation album King of the Delta Blues Singers.

1

A Devilish Deal

Early in his career, itinerant musician Robert Leroy Johnson had, by most standards, a meteoric rise from mediocre guitar player to the heights of musical genius. And thus, a myth was born: Robert Johnson cut a deal with the Devil at the crossroads of Highways 49 and 61 in Clarksdale, Mississippi. Johnson handed over his guitar. The Devil tuned it, played a few songs, and returned the instrument to its owner. During the exchange, Johnson gained mastery of his guitar and was crowned "King of the Delta Blues." The Devil's only requirement in return? Johnson's immortal soul.

It's an odd tale about an odd man, who lived a brief twenty-seven years (1911-38) but whose everlasting spirit has had an indelible impact on music notables such as Eric Clapton, Bob Dylan, and Keith Richards of the Rolling Stones. On hearing a Johnson recording for the first time, Robert Plant of Led Zeppelin declared that Robert Johnson was the man to whom all musicians owed their very existence. In 1961, a rediscovery of Johnson's early recordings led Columbia Records to release a compilation of his music, *King of the Delta Blues Singers*. Thirty years later Columbia released *The Complete Recordings*. This album sold more than one million copies and won a Grammy for Best Historical Album. In 1994, the United States Post Office issued a postage stamp with Johnson's likeness, memorializing the musician as a national icon.

Yet, mystery continues to surround the life of Robert Johnson. In their biography of him, *Robert Johnson: Lost and Found*, authors Barry Lee Pearson and Bill McCulloch wrote that Johnson originally trained on a diddley bow—one or more strings nailed taut to the side of a barn—

and that he wasn't much of a guitar player in his youth. A later mentor, musician Son House, remembered Johnson as a little boy—a competent harmonica player but an embarrassingly bad guitarist. House also cited Johnson's disastrous attempts to perform as an adult. In an interview, Son shared that when Johnson would commandeer a stage during intermissions, he was met with howls from the audience. Johnson then purportedly left town, only to reemerge six months later as a superstar. "He was so good!" exclaimed an astonished House. "When he finished all our mouths were standing open." Tales followed that it was during this very six-month absence that Johnson made his unholy alliance with the Devil. How else, those in the community speculated, to account for Johnson's rapid mastery of the guitar? How else to explain Johnson's newfound ability to play in a wide range of styles, from raw country slide guitar, to jazz and pop licks, to uptown swing and ragtime?

On first hearing a Johnson recording, guitarist Keith Richards of Rolling Stones fame asked, "Who's the other guy playing with him?" When told it was just Johnson, Richards said, "I was hearing two guitars, and it took me a long time to realize, he was actually doing it all by himself. . . . Robert Johnson was like an orchestra all by himself." And none other than Eric Clapton described Johnson's accompanying vocals as "the most powerful cry that I think you can find in the human voice."

Even Johnson's lyrics hint at a devilish connection. Although his plaintive song "Hellhound On My Trail" is a lament about a woman, the opening lyrics speak to a need to outrace or outwit an otherworldly entity.

> *I got to keep movin', I got to keep movin'*
> *Blues fallin' down like hail, blues fallin' down like hail*
> *Hmm-mmm, blues fallin' down like hail, blues fallin' down like hail*
> *And the days keeps on worryin' me*
> *There's a hellhound on my trail, hellhound on my trail*
> *Hellhound on my trail*

Other scholars, musicologists, family, and friends debunk the deal-with-the-Devil myth. They claim that Johnson's life story is but a reflection of the times: the legacy of an African-American male in the segregated South. Even as a child, Robert led a nomadic life. Robert

Johnson was born in May 1911 in Hazlehurst, Mississippi to Julia Major Dodds, married to Charles Dodds. Charles fled a lynch mob, changed his surname to Spencer, and settled in Memphis, where Julia eventually took baby Robert Dodds. For the next eight to nine years in Memphis, Robert (Dodds) Spencer attended the Carnes Avenue Colored School. Around 1919, Robert rejoined his mother in Arkansas, where she had married a sharecropper named Will "Dusty" Willis. They soon moved near Tunica, Mississippi, where Robert Dodds Spencer was known to locals as "Little Robert Dusty," but he retained the name of Robert Spencer while attending Tunica's Indian Creek School.

In February of 1929, when Robert Dodds Spencer Willis married sixteen-year-old Virginia Travis, his mother told him his biological father was actually a man named Noah Johnson, whom she had met during her marriage to Charles Dodds. Robert chose to adopt the surname of Johnson, using it on his marriage certificate. Sadly for the newlyweds, Virginia died in childbirth, as did the child. Years later, Virginia's surviving relatives stated that the deaths of mother and child were Robert's fault: divine punishment for singing secular songs, known at the time as "selling your soul to the Devil." Blues researcher Robert McCormick believed that Johnson accepted this as his fate for his refusal to settle into life as a husband and farmer and choosing instead to become a full-time blues musician.

One strong influence in Robert's young life was Mississippi guitarist Isaiah "Ike" Zimmerman. With him the Devil myth would take on new proportions, as the two were known to play for the dead in graveyards at midnight. As a teenager, Robert slipped into the Mississippi town of Robinsonville with its popular juke joints and heard performances by Delta blues pioneer Son House. But mostly, say Johnson's defenders, his true talent came from a combination of practice to hone his craft and an innate ability to play any song after hearing it just once.

During his "transformation" or, as some believed, pact with the Devil, Johnson lived in the Delta town of Martinsville, where he fathered a child by Vergie Mae Smith, but married Caletta Craft in 1931. By 1933, Robert Johnson left for a career as a "walking" or itinerant musician. He played on street corners and in restaurants, barbershops, and juke joints, moving frequently from Memphis to the smaller towns of the

Mississippi Delta, with occasional forays into Illinois, Texas, New York, Canada, Kentucky, and Indiana. He was said to have a woman in every town that he'd seduced at each performance. Perhaps following his childhood existence, Johnson used different names in each town with aliases in excess of eight surnames.

His luck ran out, however, at a performance near Greenwood, Mississippi. He died on August 16, 1938, at the age of twenty-seven. His death certificate went missing until musicologist Gayle Dean Wardlow discovered it almost thirty years later. No official cause of death was noted, although, due to his lifestyle, syphilis was suspected. Then local oral tradition took over. One theory was that Johnson was murdered by the jealous husband of a woman with whom he flirted. The woman unknowingly gave Johnson a bottle of whiskey poisoned by her husband. Johnson began to feel ill. Over the next three days, his condition worsened. Witnesses reported that Johnson died in a "convulsive state of severe pain." Bruce Conforth and Gayle Dean Wardlow, in their book *Up Jumped the Devil*, believe that the poison was naphthalene made from dissolved mothballs, a "common way of poisoning people in the rural South."

Even if Robert Leroy Johnson made a deal with the Devil to raise his musical talents to the level of genius, he neglected to include a note about shielding himself from harm. And the world lost, in the words of Eric Clapton, "the most important blues musician who ever lived."

Music is a powerful conduit to connect with the past. In the deep rich Delta region of Mississippi, the spirit of the "King of the Delta Blues," Robert Leroy Johnson, lives on through his plaintive voice and guitar riffs to inspire new legends.

Lagniappe: The riddle that was Robert Leroy Johnson continues in the afterlife. Markers have been erected at three different locations; all purport to be his final resting place. Johnson's death certificate named "Zion Church," but that was little help as there are at least three churches in the area using the word "Zion." Research in the 1980s through the 1990s suggested that Johnson's remains lie buried at the Mount Zion Missionary Baptist Church near Morgan City, near Greenwood. A one-ton obelisk lists all of his songs. Placed in the church's cemetery in 1990, it

Mystery surrounds the final resting place of Robert Johnson. This marker is at the Little Zion Church near Greenwood.

was paid for by Columbia Records and through smaller contributions to the Mt. Zion Memorial Fund. Also in 1990, a small rectangular marker with the epitaph *Resting in the Blues* was placed in the cemetery of Payne Chapel, not far from Quito, Mississippi. The Atlanta rock group the Tombstones saw a photograph of an unmarked spot alleged by one of Johnson's ex-girlfriends to be his burial site and took action. Finally, the Little Zion Church, on Money Road near Greenwood, claims that Johnson is buried under a great pecan tree in the church cemetery, based on a 2000 statement by Rosie Eskridge, wife of the supposed gravedigger. Sony Music placed a marker there. This location was verified by Johnson's half-sister, Carrie Spencer Harris, who on learning of her brother's hasty burial in a homemade coffin hired the area's only Black undertaker to reinter Johnson in a professionally made casket. The undertaker, one Paul McDonald, kept records listing the Little Zion Church as Johnson's final resting place.

There is yet a fourth site to be considered. In his documentary, *The Search for Robert Johnson* (1991), John Hammond, Jr., suggests that, due to extreme poverty and lack of transportation, Robert Leroy Johnson was likely buried in an unmarked pauper's grave near where he died. But despite the legends swirling around Robert Leroy Johnson, his grandson, Steven Johnson, president of the Robert Johnson Blues Foundation, just wants the truth to be told. "That's my heritage. That's my bloodline." At the same time, he has not asked for any of the markers to be removed. He appreciates that his grandfather's fans enjoy the mystery, and he hopes that the "ghost stories" and tales of sorcery—the collusion with the Devil—will one day yield to the flesh-and-blood reality that was Robert Leroy Johnson, "King of the Delta Blues."

2

The Mystery of the Masked Marvel

Charley Patton—"Father of the Delta Blues," "Voice of the Delta," "The Masked Marvel"—died April 28, 1934, and was buried quickly at his own request. "He died that Saturday, and we buried him that Sunday, 'cause he didn't want to go to an undertaker," said his niece, Bessie Turner. Sometime after 1934, Vocalion Records erected a marker in Longswitch Cemetery. However, at least one local resident argued that the marker was in the wrong place.

In the early 1990s there was a movement to honor blues legends and rescue rural Black churches and cemeteries. Skip Henderson, founder of the Mt. Zion Memorial Fund, was quoted as saying in a 2018 article for *Mississippi Folklife,* "It's about saving the soul of Mississippi." This same article ("Charley Patton's Grave: More than a Memorial in Holly Ridge," by T. DeWayne Moore) repeats an oft-told tale. Two researchers doubted the placement of the original grave marker was correct and went searching for Charley's remains. In 1980, on a stormy day near sundown with thunder roaring and flashes of lightning scarring the sky, one of the men "felt a distinct chill come over his body in the far left corner of the graveyard."

The researchers, some say, had intuitively stumbled on the correct gravesite. Meanwhile others, who believe in the ability of the long dead to communicate with the living, were certain it was the voice of Charley calling out to them. The "new" location of the unmarked grave was confirmed by Joseph "Cootchie" Howard, longtime cemetery caretaker. Howard recalled that contractors had accidentally removed Charley Patton's remains when expanding a nearby cotton gin. The blues musician's

The "Voice of the Delta," Charley Patton, led a nomadic life mired in personal struggles.

final resting place lay ignominiously underneath the site of the gin's lint incinerator, which had blown down during a storm.

To add to the grim location, Patton's unmarked grave was surrounded by a pile of waste from the cotton gin. On July 20, 1991, Henderson and *Living Blues* magazine founder Jim O'Neal rectified the disgraceful situation. At the Holly Ridge Cemetery (the old Longswitch Cemetery), they honored Charley Patton. A new gravestone was installed bearing Charley's name and the legend *The Voice of the Delta*. In attendance were Patton's daughter, Rosetta Patton Brown, and numerous grandchildren and great-grandchildren. Whether Charley's restless spirit chimed in to aid in the search for his remains is woven into the mystery of the Mississippi Delta.

In 1991, the genius that was Charley Patton was finally honored with a new gravestone at Holly Ridge Cemetery.

Whatever the impetus that led to the newly installed grave marker, Charles Patton, the "Father of the Delta Blues," finally received his due. In 2007 Charley's gravesite in Holly Ridge, Mississippi was the first to receive a marker on the Mississippi Blues Trail. As the first blues superstar, Patton's musical influence spread to gospel, R&B, and rock and roll. John Fogerty, lead singer, lead guitarist, and founder of the band Creedence Clearwater Revival, stated, "When I discovered that Patton was the root of it all [the Delta blues], I came here to Holly Ridge last year [1990]. It was then I first put a Patton tape in my boom box and when I heard his voice, it sounded like Moses."

Charley Patton's life, like the blues musicians who followed him, was mired in personal struggles. Born to Bill and Annie Patton around 1891, Charley was drawn to music, but his religious parents felt that music, especially playing secular songs on guitar, was sinful. Throughout his life, Charley lived a dual existence. Known to be a hard-drinking womanizer, he also clung to his roots as a God-fearing preacher. According to niece Bessie Turner, days before his death, Charley said to her, "Count my Christian records and count my swinging records. Just count 'em. They even!" In his 2002 review of Patton's music for *Musical Traditions Magazine,* Fred McCormick pointed to Patton's wide-ranging repertoire with ballads ("Frankie and Albert"), minstrel songs ("Love My Stuff"), and spirituals ("Lord, I'm Discouraged," "I Shall Not Be Moved"). "Charley Patton uses the blues as a vehicle for documenting his own intensely personal experiences. He seems to live the songs he is singing."

Charley's background is also a source for conjecture. Said to be a blend of African-American, Native American, and White ancestry, he was married an astonishing eight times, with Bertha Lee Patton (with whom he performed) as his final wife. Starting in 1910, Charley reputedly traveled the New Orleans-Memphis-Chicago circuit. By 1914, at the age of twenty-three, he was making his living as a musician. He made his first recordings in 1929. Ethnomusicologist David Evans christened Charley the first "star" of the Delta blues. Evans went on to explain that Charley "served as a role model for a whole way of life—by being independent, traveling and cutting records at a time when nobody expected men like him to go anywhere."

On the day of the ceremony honoring Charley at the Holly Ridge

Cemetery, the Reverend Ernest Ware declared, "Charley Patton made the way for us." Charley Patton died near Indianola, Mississippi on April 28, 1934, of heart disease shortly after returning from his final recording session. Through his recordings, his voice continues to both haunt and inspire.

Lagniappe: Paramount Records promoted Charley Patton under various aliases in an unusually styled media campaign. For the release of "Pony Blues" coupled with "Banty Rooster Blues," he was Charley Patton, country blues wizard. With "Prayer of Death" (Parts 1 and 2) Charley became Elder J. J. Hadley, to keep the focus on the songs' more spiritual nature. For Charley's third release, "Mississippi Boweavil Blues" and "Screamin' and Hollerin' the Blues," Charley became "The Masked Marvel." As part of the advertising hype, potential buyers were invited to guess: who was this masked man? If they got it right, Paramount offered a prize of another Paramount Record of their choice. The "Masked Marvel" moniker was a bit of creative marketing carried to the extreme. Although Charley was certainly a musical marvel, at no time did he ever take up wearing a Zorro-like mask. Despite the misleading gimmick, the ploy worked. The recording sold 5,000 copies, a high number for a blues recording at that time. Unfortunately, no documents have been found tallying how many buyers correctly guessed that Charley Patton was "The Masked Marvel"—the man behind the music.

Music reviewer Fred McCormick speculated on what it must have felt like to see and hear Charley in person. "He was an exciting performer, and an evening spent dancing to Charley Patton screaming and hollering the blues must have been one hell of a way of discharging the frustrations of life, as good as getting your sins washed away in the tide."

The Old Armory, now Washington County's Convention and Visitors Bureau.

3

The Whistler

Greenville bills itself as the "Heart and Soul of the Delta." Recently, a few old souls felt compelled to reappear. As the seat of Washington County, Greenville has a storied past, reflected in her historic homes, schools, churches, cemeteries, and commercial structures. There is a timeless quality to it all, a mystique, and a new restlessness that the long dead have not entirely left the premises.

Just a block off the Mississippi River, the old National Guard Armory has been repurposed as the offices of the Washington County Convention and Visitors Bureau. Unfazed by walls decorated with colorful posters promoting the area's cultural attractions, one former guardsman remains on duty.

Wesley Smith, the energetic director of the bureau, has seen the soldier on patrol. "I got here in October of 2008; a month later, in November, I was leaving for the night. The rest of the staff was gone. I got up from my desk, closed the door to my office, went halfway down the center hall to cut off the light switches, and in a split second, there he was." Smith gets up to demonstrate. "I was heading forward towards the front of the building." Smith points to the double metal doors that serve as the entrance. Each has a clear glass panel in the upper half. "It was already dark outside, so with the light inside, the windows in the doors acted like mirrors. Just as I was thinking that I need to cut the lights out, I see in the reflection of the glass panels a man in uniform walk across the hall behind me." Smith's voice rises. "It wasn't a wisp or anything; it was a solid-looking man. He didn't look at me; [he] just kept going out of what I thought was a door at the end of the hall and into the wall on the opposite side." Smith admits the sight startled him. "My first thought was that my brain had somehow transposed something. I couldn't be seeing what I was seeing, and I'd gotten confused." Rushing to make sense of what was happening, he bolted for the front door. "I pulled it open and scanned the street up and down. We don't get much street traffic here, let alone someone walking after hours. It was dark, and there was a light rain . . . and the street was empty."

The youthful-looking director makes it clear that until that moment, haunted tales had not easily swayed him. "I had never seen a ghost before. I'd never even taken a position one way or another if spirits, ghosts can return." Smith is positive of two things: the figure of a man appeared *behind* him, and he was in uniform. "It was an early World War II style with a long, light-colored tunic belted at the waist, and the pants were baggy around his upper legs and then tapered below his knees." These tapered pants were first worn by cavalry units so there would be less material to tuck into their boots while on horseback.

As news of the incident spread, people in Greenville came forward to share photos, souvenirs, and memories. "A man named Tommy Harmon, whose father was stationed here for years, brought us a commemorative book from 1938. When I saw the pictures, I got goose bumps. There in the photos was the exact uniform." The man who shared the book also shared another detail in support of Smith's ghostly visitor. "Oddly enough, when we walked to the rear of the hallway and I showed him where the soldier crossed, Tommy pointed out that where the wall is solid now, there used to be a doorway. You can see the outline where it's been bricked up. I thought it was kinda neat that the soldier could have come out of the old doorway."

Originally, the squat, solid structure on Walnut Street was part of a 1930 army base before becoming the headquarters for Battery A, First Battalion, 114th Field Artillery of the Mississippi National Guard. On December 13, 1959, it was rededicated as Fort Nicholson to honor Louis M. Nicholson Jr. of Greenville, killed in action in 1943. The armory served as headquarters for the Second Reconnaissance Squadron, 198th Armor, Thirty-first Infantry (Dixie) Division. Commissioned officers, noncommissioned officers, sergeants, corporals, and privates have all drilled here. The echoes of their footsteps have occasionally interrupted the daily routines of the current occupants.

The morning after Smith spotted the soldier, he checked in with the bureau's other staff members. "I said to Lisa and Catherine, 'Have you ever seen or heard anything strange?' And they both looked at me and then at each other. I go, 'I've only been here a month. Tell me, what?'"

Lisa Winters is Smith's executive assistant. Her charming personality bubbles over. She speaks frankly about the ghostly activity in the old armory. "The footsteps overhead sound more like the thuds that boots make rather than shoes." Winters leads a tour through the vacant second floor. Large metal cabinets, some resting on their backs, others propped on their sides; discarded wooden crates; and unidentified objects swathed in layers of dust, a graveyard of the forgotten, create a forlorn scene. Winters keeps up a running commentary. "We've heard stuff up here." She looks down on two parallel skid marks on the dusty floor. "See, those marks are fresh. It's as if someone dragged one of the cabinets across the floor. And we hear heavy thuds like the boxes are being picked up in the air and then dropped. Catherine and I both hear it, but she doesn't like to talk about it much." Winters stands with her hands on her hips and surveys the room. "Why would anybody want to be up here?" She wipes the sweat dripping from her forehead with the back of her hand. "We had some ghost hunters here awhile back and it was just like this—about one hundred degrees. They had these temperature gauges going in this room and immediately the temperature dropped like twenty degrees. There's no air-conditioning here. And you can see how the sun just beats through these large windows. The ghost hunters say cold spots are the sign that a spirit is around." Winters grins. "I don't know anything about that."

The front of the armory faces the old Greenville Inn and Suites. To the right is a parking lot. Winters looks out the window to her red car parked below. "When I'm the last one to leave, I lock up, and as I cross the street, it feels like someone is staring down at me from this upstairs window, but when I turn around, no one is there." Winters, her blue-green eyes shining under a cap of blond hair, is glad of one thing: "I'm not alone when it comes to hearing some of these things."

The executive assistant has rejoined the director in his office. She peers across the wide expanse of desk to Smith, seeking confirmation. "What really got both of us was the whistling." Smith stretches his slender frame back in his chair, and lets Winters begin.

"I was typing at the computer and there was this really loud whistling.

I thought it was Wesley, and I said to myself, 'Well, I guess Wesley is in a really good mood.'" As the whistling continued, Winters heard the outer side door open and close. Smith entered the building.

"I didn't hear anything outside," says Smith, "but when I stepped in, I could hear this melody. I couldn't tell you the song, but it had form, like a military tune. I got about halfway up the hall, and I called out, 'Lisa, is that you?' I turned into her office and she jumped."

"My heart sank." There is a quiver in Winters' drawl.

"She thought it was me and I thought it was her."

And the ghost of the old armory probably had a good chuckle.

Another incident had a bit of an intimidation factor. On this day, Lisa Winters and fellow staff member Catherine Gardner were assembled in Smith's office. "Catherine was seated where Lisa is now in front of my desk, and Lisa was standing closer to the doorway." Smith relates the sequence of events as they occurred during the informal meeting: "I had my legs crossed and propped up on the desk. We had been in there about ten minutes, having this long conversation and all of a sudden, I hear over my shoulder: 'Haaaar.'" Smith lifts his right shoulder up to his ear as if to banish the unwelcomed sound. "It was so loud, all three of us heard it at the same time, and we all jumped."

"I heard it over here by me, and Catherine thought it was coming from behind her like someone was breathing heavy," adds Winters.

"It came out like an explosion. 'Haaaar.'" Smith repeats the sound.

The staff at the Washington Convention and Visitors Bureau are uncertain if they have one ghost or a rotating cadre of spirits. A veteran in the community votes for the single ghost theory. Reports of the ongoing paranormal activity at the armory prompted retired S.Sgt. C. J. Coursey to write a letter to the editor of the *Delta Times Democrat*. In the letter, Coursey states that neither during his years of service nor his father's was there was any talk of ghosts at the armory. The retired sergeant speculates that the hauntings did not start until after the armory was abandoned by the military. Coursey refers to a thank-you proclamation hanging in the city library. "It was signed by all or most of them soldiers. My father's name is there and so is the man I suspect to be the ghost." The letter writer goes on to say that the alleged ghost was a noncommissioned officer who rose to the rank of command sergeant major. In 1990, the

National Guard unit at Fort Nicholson was activated for Desert Storm, but the senior noncommissioned officer was not deployed due to his age. "The state of Mississippi hired this old soldier to watch over the property," says Coursey. "He probably did not like being left behind after all the years of being in charge."

After the unit returned, the headquarters moved into to a new facility and the old armory building was donated to the city of Greenville. Coursey feels his former commander never accepted the change. "I suspect this guy is in that building and really needs, big time, to report to the supreme commander." And, according to Coursey, the task will be monumental. "It may take . . . all of us living old soldiers to convince this man/ghost that his work is done on this planet."

Some residents of Greenville believe that this statue can talk.

Lagniappe: The bronze statue of another warrior adds a twist to Greenville's haunted lore. The large figure of a medieval knight stands with his metal-mesh-gloved hands leaning on the handle of his sword. Greenville writer William Alexander Percy erected the stoic knight as a memorial to his father, LeRoy Percy (1860-1929), a former senator and planter. In his feature film *Home Again* for the Washington County Convention and Visitors Bureau, broadcaster and lifelong resident Walt Grayson reflects on the statue's ghostly ability to speak. According to Grayson, as kids they were told that if you placed your hands on top of the statue's folded ones, looked directly in to its eyes, and asked, "What are you doing here?" the statue would respond, "Absolutely nothing." Grayson sardonically adds, "It is still doing nothing as far as I can tell." The "talking" statue was a popular stop on the 2021 Greenville Cemetery tour, "Monuments on Main Street."

4

More Greenville Ghosts

At the former E. E. Bass Junior High School in Greenville, there is another old timer too dedicated to leave. Herman Solomon was the principal for more than twenty-five years from the 1940s through the 1960s. The school he presided over was a mammoth complex. Built in two phases, the original Greenville High School was completed in 1916. In 1929, the junior-high annex was designed by renowned architect A. Hays Town. Both schools became the educational center of Greenville. Death has not deterred a vigilant principal from making his rounds.

"Those who have seen his ghost say it strolls the halls, which he did." Warren Harper attended E. E. Bass School from 1959 to 1964. His memories of Herman Solomon are vivid. "Principal Solomon was a gnomish figure, a real small man who made a big impression. To us middle schoolers, he was a holy terror." In the hindsight of age, Harper acknowledges that Solomon was a good old disciplinarian. "He was hands on, but he didn't whip your fanny; he just sent you to the coach."

In 1980, due to age and increasing maintenance costs, the school closed its doors. Members of the community banded together to form the E. E. Bass Foundation to salvage the auditorium for performance space and turn other portions into offices. The attempts were only partially successful. For the next fifteen years, the vacant red brick building with its Grecian-style columns took on a mournful appearance. Sections of the roof collapsed and rumors of hauntings began to circulate.

"The first sightings were in the early to mid-1990s," says Harper. Harper is a founding member of Delta Center Stage, a local theatre group that began to restore the once lavish auditorium. "We came in

31

A former principal still walks the halls of E. E. Bass Junior High School.

here in 1991. The place was a maintenance nightmare. Beyond the auditorium, there was no electricity, and when you came down the halls, it was dark. It was like a cave, a very, very spooky place, especially in the evenings." Harper concedes that the theatre troupe members probably scared each other as they crawled all over the space not knowing who was where. "On the second floor," says Harper, "you always had the feeling that someone was watching you. When we first came in the building, there were feral cats who had taken over, so there were always these eerie scratching sounds." Harper remembers one evening when his hair "stood on end." "There was a costume party and I was late. I had to go upstairs to the costume room by myself and I had to use a flashlight. This soft, scratching sound starts. I couldn't figure out if the scratcher had four legs or two legs . . . or even a body at all, so I grabbed a costume and got out of there."

Warren Harper has never seen the ghost, but the two people who have both swear that when they spotted the short male figure in the hall, he was walking away from them, lost in thought as if he didn't even know they were there. Harper surmises that the former principal was probably more focused on finding his students. "If ever a spirit should be haunting this building, it's got to be Herman Solomon. He loved this place. This was his life."

In downtown Greenville in a red brick building once teeming with life, a despondent reporter decided that life was not worth living. His troubled spirit appears on the upper floor of the historic *Delta Democrat Times* newspaper office.

An unhappy spirit haunts the second floor of the original Delta Democrat Times *building.*

The *Delta Democrat Times* newspaper rose to fame under the leadership of Hodding Carter II. In 1946, Carter won the Pulitzer Prize for his editorials advocating racial tolerance and his series lambasting the ill treatment of Japanese-American soldiers returning from World War II. Today, the newspaper operates out of quarters on North Broadway Street. The original site, on the corner of Walnut and Main, is a hollow shell. The only living occupant is metal artist John "Puddin'" Moore.

Puddin' crafts fish, butterflies, and swamp scenes out of scrap metal found along the levee. He works in the garage annex attached to the back of the old newspaper offices. This skilled sculptor is familiar with the history of the building and has no issue sharing space with any of its ghosts. "I hear bumps and noises and all kinds of things up there, but I don't pay no attention to it. This place has been a lot of different things— newspaper office, funeral home, furniture company, paint store—so it's hard to tell who the ghost might have been." Puddin' works as he talks, shifting sheets of metal on two scarred, wooden tables. A crumbling brick wall separates his studio space from the main structure.

Puddin' is a wiry man who moves deftly through the years of accumulated debris. He leads the way up a back staircase into a barren, cavernous second-floor room. Bare light sockets dangle fifteen feet from the ceiling on black electrical cords. "The newspaper moved out of here in 1967. It's spooky up here. Used to be where they had the printing presses, typeset everything by hand." The trapped heat is oppressive. The artist saunters over to a large freight elevator along the rear wall.

Running gnarled fingers through the thick wedge of white hair splayed over his forehead, he spins off a tale of a gruesome encounter. "See, back when the newspaper was still here, there was a custodian. They usually worked in groups of two or three, but that night he was by himself. He came up the freight elevator, stepped out of the door, and the ghost was staring back at him. The old man ghost was in all white, like a shroud." Puddin' says the only color on the figure was a long gray beard. "That guy, after he saw the ghost, he dropped everything, flew out the door, and down the street. He called the editor and said, 'If you want the building locked up, you'd better send somebody else because I am not going back up there.' He said, 'I wasn't seeing things either because this old man just stood perfectly still and stared at me.'"

The entrance to the Delta Democrat Times.

Puddin' gives a whirlwind tour of the building. The curving front stairwell ends halfway down. Skeletal pigeon and other unidentifiable animal remains, rotting steps, and fallen slates from the ceiling barricade the descent. Mold makes breathing difficult. Puddin' offers to hoist the freight elevator, operated by a series of ropes and weights. I gave him a negative response, and we return to the ground floor via the relatively clutter free rear staircase.

More detritus awaits. A sixteen-foot boat, complete with outboard motor, is parked on a trailer. In the back corner, broken pieces of furniture are piled to the ceiling. It is hard to imagine that the legendary newspaperman Hodding Carter ever worked out of this space. Puddin' waves his arms and draws a picture of a room once humming with the click of typewriter keys. "There were cubbyholes all over here, and the editor had his own office back there." He indicates another spot under a bank of windows. "One guy who worked here found out his wife cheated on him, and he blew his brains out. Might be that's his ghost upstairs." Puddin' delivers this bit of shocking news as he ambles off to the garage to point out the high water mark from the 1927 flood that inundated Greenville.

Back in his studio, this artist and collector shows off the bottles, arrowheads, and bones he has scavenged from the riverbanks. A true Greenville character, Puddin' is as comfortable with the ghosts of the old *Delta Democrat Times* building as he is with his artifacts. "Been here twenty-five years; nothing surprises me."

Lagniappe: The Mississippi Delta also holds bragging rights to a teddy bear and a frog. At South Main and Crescent streets, a historic marker in the Live Oak Cemetery leads to the tale of a presidential bear. In 1902, Theodore Roosevelt arrived in the Delta for a much-anticipated hunting expedition. By the light of a campfire, Holt Collier, the "greatest bear hunter of all time," promised to capture a bear for the president. Collier delivered, but an empathetic Roosevelt couldn't shoot. Roosevelt's failure to shoot was satirized in a political cartoon. Inspired by the president's sympathy for the bear, a toy maker created the now immortal "Teddy Bears." The cuddly bears began with Holt Collier and a presidential visit to the Delta.

Just down Highway 82 in Leland, another Mississippi native son created one of the most popular children's characters of all time. As a child, Muppet master Jim Henson played along the banks of Deer Creek. The frolicking swamp creatures captured the child's imagination. He ran home, tore up an old coat of his mother's, cut a ping pong ball in half for

The author with Kermit the Frog at the Jim Henson Museum in Leland.

eyes, and Kermit the Frog arrived on the scene. The Washington Country Welcome Center displays an original Kermit and offers an opportunity to pose with a larger-than-life-sized version of the beloved green Muppet.

Legendary characters, real or imagined, warm and fuzzy, or spectral and spooky, thrive in Greenville, the timeless "Heart and Soul of the Delta."

5

Lake Washington's Lonely Spirits

Eighteen miles south of Greenville lies one of the most serene and ancient lakes in the Delta. Seven hundred years ago, when the mighty Mississippi changed course, it created an oxbow lake. Two separate bends in the river merged to form Lake Washington. Before the lake was formally named, Native American tribes, such as the Choctaws, camped on its banks and enjoyed its abundant hunting and fishing grounds.

One Choctaw guide is said to have shown this natural wonder to Indian agent Robert Ward. In 1825, Ward purchased 2,000 acres for fifty dollars in gold. His transaction brought White settlers to the region. Wealthy planters with impressive lineages, including Hezekiah William Foote, Frederick G. Turnball, Scotsman S. M. Spencer, Wade Hampton, and Henry and Elizabeth Johnson, recognized the potential of the fertile delta soil. Cotton plantations spread out across the eastern shores and small villages emerged.

Today, the glory days are gone. Village stores are shuttered. The magnificent mansions of the cotton barons are reduced to a footnote in history. Along East Lake Washington Road—more shell pathway than paved roadway—two faded ladies are the last holdouts of an unprecedented era. Their haunted appearances fuel ghost tales passed from generation to generation in the tiny hamlet of Glen Allan.

On a searing hot day in late August, the mirrored surface of Lake Washington is stretched taut and still. The bluegill, crappie, and catfish have retreated to its cool depths. The parched brown branches of the cypress trees are scorched to their tips. Only the cicadas seem to take a perverse joy in the oxygen-depleted air. Their spirited singing is disorienting. As the males contract their internal timbal muscles, their hollow stomachs amplify the clicking noises, virtually drowning out the voices of the humans gathered below the trees.

Mike Jones, a local fishing guide and owner of Bait n' Thangs Tackle Shop, wipes the sweat raining down from his forehead. He is conflicted. Standing by a side entrance to the crumbling Mt. Holly Plantation house, he wants people to appreciate this lonely remnant of the Delta's history, but he won't cross the threshold. His fear does not stem from any physical danger inside the deteriorating structure. Rather it is a deep-down-gut-induced warning that whatever lurks inside is not warm and friendly. "I listen to my instincts. You don't have to worry about me going no further. Ain't going to happen."

With his broad, barrel chest; curling biceps; and bristly white beard, Jones could easily slip into frontier garb and walk among the early settlers. His physical presence is imposing; the unacquainted might hold

Mt. Holly waits to be rescued on the shores of Lake Washington.

back. Yet he speaks with a gentle voice, filled with genuine warmth. Jones checks up periodically on the condition of the abandoned plantation built in 1856 by Margaret Johnson Erwin. He has no idea if it was Margaret's annoyed spirit who slammed the door in his face on an earlier visit; however, he does take the action to heart.

The incident occurred when Jones had escorted two women to the site on the lake's eastern shore. Both women were interested in preserving the historic home described as one of the finest examples of Italianate Villa architecture. They had circled past the large side veranda and were near the old kitchen annex, which juts out in the back. An arched walkway runs along one side of the house. The covered passageway had been enclosed with panes of glass during its conversion into a bed and breakfast. Jones' eyes close into slits as he recalls the episode.

On that morning, a single wooden door leading to the kitchen space is ajar. The two women enter first. Jones steps up to follow, only to have the door fly into his face with a vengeance. He stumbles backwards. As he makes his retreat, he spies the fleeting shape of a woman running down the passageway next to the kitchen.

Jones is firm in his conviction that the figure he saw was not human. Although the apparition was transparent, there was enough of a form for him to know that the door-slammer was female. Despite the ghost's rejection, Jones rarely turns down requests to guide interested parties to Mt. Holly. "History is a big thing with me. I hate having this place run down like this."

Mt. Holly is fading fast. The carved balusters on the balconies have been battered by the elements; those that remain are nearly stripped of their decorative paint and bleached to a dull gray. Windowpanes are broken or missing entirely. Most alarming is the condition of the red clay brick. Chunks have disintegrated, undermining the integrity of the columns and the exterior walls. One preservationist source attributes the loss to "incorrect maintenance by a previous owner in the 1970-1980s." In an attempt to repoint the brick, the original lime mortar, which naturally breathes with the soft bricks, was replaced with a cement-based mortar that can't react to the change in seasons. The missing sections of brick look as if some monster hand has reached in and clawed out random chunks.

Also at odds with the historic façade are the more contemporary screen doors that hang off-kilter. The radical angle of the screens makes the double front doors behind them appear as if they too are leaning away from the house. On the roof, the leftover scraps of dingy white tarp finish off the distressed, haunted house appearance. The tarp fragments dangle limply from the eaves—torn shrouds pierced with nails—offering no function other than to add another layer of disgraceful neglect. On moonlit nights, with a light breeze lifting the tattered scraps, the effect is that of a thousand shrouded spirits dancing on the roof.

Mike Jones had also visited Mt. Holly in its waning days of human occupation. After the family of Margaret Johnson had moved out, the thirty-two rooms were renovated as an upscale bed-and breakfast-retreat. After this commercial enterprise failed, the then-owners rented it out for weddings and other special occasions. A few area businesses—caterers, florists, and rental supply companies—benefited from the mansion's continued, if sporadic, use.

In addition to his tackle shop and RV campgrounds on the lake, Jones also operates a Christmas tree farm. The last time he actually ventured inside Mt. Holly was the day he delivered Christmas trees as part of the décor for a wedding ceremony at the mansion. "They were setting up right inside the lobby there, by that front parlor, and that's as far as I've ever been." Jones says that he set up his trees on stands as quickly as he could and got out. When asked why he was never curious to see more of the home, and why he planned on a quick exit, his reply is succinct: "You get that eerie feeling that someone or something is watching you, and you get out. If you're uncomfortable somewhere, you leave."

Other curious souls, who happen to come upon the neglected home, have described more pleasant encounters. One traveler from Louisiana wrote on her blog that after poking around and peering in windows, she is positive she heard music coming from the old piano and the soft sounds of laughter.

Reports have circulated that the current owner, who purchased the house in 2001, lives in Texas and his plans for the property are uncertain. Within the past few years, a house trailer was moved to the grounds. It sits at edge of the front lawn, obscuring the view of the house from the lake. Workers lived there temporarily, started repairs, and left. The trailer, like the grand lady behind it, also shows signs of vandalism and neglect.

Visitors have heard music coming from the abandoned piano in the parlor.

If the ghost of original owner Margaret Johnson does return, she would likely be appalled. Floral wallpaper hangs in ragged strips. The stunning rosewood staircase with its trumpet balusters is littered with debris, making passage upwards impossible. Sections of the intricate plaster friezes, lining the fourteen-foot ceilings, and the carved medallions over the chandeliers have crashed to the floor. Curiously, the glass-and-bronze chandeliers and the marble mantels in the dining room and parlor have survived. The library's floor-to-ceiling shelves are lined with books, their condition unknown. In the pink front room, a massive antique mahogany piano is shoved against the interior wall. In such unstable conditions of heat, humidity, and cold, if ghostly fingers do run over the warped keys, as has been reported by a few visitors and backed by local rumors, the resulting sound would have to be horrific.

Recently, reporter and webmaster Woodrow "Woody" Wilkins of CBS-affiliate WXVT-Delta News arrived on the scene to file a report.

Peeling wallpaper inside Mt. Holly.

Following interviews with Mike Jones and me, Wilkins shifted the camera to his shoulder and circled the grounds to shoot additional footage of the exterior. Upon completing his circuit, Wilkins returned and stood underneath the Palladian-style front archway. He lowered his camera to the ground and made two announcements. While shooting in the rear, he turned around to get a shot of the wooded area in back. As he did, a sudden sound, like a thud or crash, came from the second floor of the house. He aimed the camera at one of the upper windows, zoomed in, and saw nothing. Wilkins grew up in the Delta and lifts his broad shoulders in dismissal. "I used to visit my sister in Jackson. We'd come up from Rolling Fork, and we could see Mt. Holly from the highway. As a child, it always had the look you'd expect from one of the old Scooby Doo cartoon haunted houses."

Jones, who has remained in the front, is staring at the wrought-iron balcony directly above Wilkins' head. Jones tells the assembled group to watch the faded curtain panel in the left front window. It is pinched about a third of the way down as if a hand has grabbed on to it. Although the air is still, the curtain moves back and forth in a rapid shaking motion. Suddenly, a welcome gust of wind lifts the strips of torn tarp on the roof. They flap in the breeze, blowing from left to right. The curtain panel stops its shaking motion and then is pulled from right to left, hugging the doorframe.

Mike Jones turns his back and heads for his black pick-up truck. He lets the bronze National Register marker have the final say.

MOUNT HOLLY
CIRCA 1856
Steeped in the history of the Mississippi Delta

It should, perhaps, more accurately read: *Steeped in the mystery of the Mississippi Delta.*

A short ride down the road from Mount Holly is the Susie B. Law House. Even Jones is shocked by its appearance—or near disappearance. An insidious, tangled mat of creeping vines envelops the entire front of the house, from ground level to hipped roof.

Now hidden by the dense overgrowth, the main architectural elements

An unseen hand shakes the curtain in the window above the balcony.

of the house are a two-story, columned portico over the front entrance; a black, wrought-iron balcony separating two sets of matching double doors, each with oval glass inserts and glass transoms; and identical bay windows on the ground floor. There is nothing left of the rear of the house. No repairs are under way. The lawn is mowed sporadically, creating a wide expanse of yellowish-brown scorched earth facing the lake. To the right, nearly crushed by the weight of the heavy vines, a miniature playhouse cries out to be rescued. The playhouse is identical in design to the big house and, in happier times, must have delighted some very pampered little girls.

In 2006, Jones was returning from Glen Allan on the way to his bait shop. "It was right before Halloween and it was raining. Nobody had been in that house since I've been here, and I've been here since 1997." Jones pinches the bridge of his nose with two fingers and shakes his head. "I was coming down the road, and I could see light inside the house. It's

Vines creep over the front of the haunted Susie B. Law House on the lake.

A playhouse is barely holding up under the weight of the vines.

all dark except for this little light going up, so I eased down. There wasn't even electricity hooked up to the house at that time. When I got to the front, there was a little ole bitty, frail lady holding a coal-oil lamp. She was climbing up the steps."

Jones is leaning against the side of his truck, arms crossed and wrapped around this chest. Back then, he explains, the vines had not spread across the house, and he had a clear view of the woman through the windows on both floors. "You could see in as plain as day. There was a real tiny lady, wearing a white dress, a nightgown kind of thing, and as best I could tell carrying an oil lamp in her hand. She had a little bun on the back of her head. When I first saw her, she was at the bottom, and I watched her go slowly up the steps all the way to the top."

"Initially, I thought it was a real person. I mean, you see the light inside a normally dark house, and you assume somebody's broken in. I am sitting there thinking, 'Who is this?' I was fixing to call the sheriff's department, and then I got to looking at her some more and I said, 'Uh, uh. Something about her ain't right.'"

Jones decided that reporting an apparition to the sheriff might not be the best idea. "So I went on and got myself away from there. Later, I told a good friend of ours, who is kin with the people, with the actual grand-daughter of Susie B. I described the lady in the house, and she checked with the family and told me that my description could fit that of the last owner—Miss Susie B." Jones nods his head sagely. "Folks have always said it was haunted. It's had that reputation every since Susie B. died."

The families who lived at Mt. Holly Plantation and the Susie B. Law House have strong interconnecting ties to Lake Washington. Indian agent Robert Ward deeded his lakefront property to his eighteen-year-old son, Julius Ward. The young Ward built Erwin House at head of the lake in 1830. One mile north of Erwin House, landowners Henry and Elizabeth Johnson ran a cotton plantation on more than 2,000 acres of land. In 1855, Henry sold part of his increased holdings of 4,000 acres to his daughter Margaret. Margaret Johnson Erwin built Mt. Holly and settled in to enjoy the expansive lake view. In the 1880s, former Confederate officer Hezekiah William Foote added Mt. Holly to his extensive holdings of Delta plantations. State senator Huger Lee Foote inherited Mt. Holly from his father. Noted author and Civil War historian Shelby

The ruins of St. John's Episcopal Church on Lake Washington.

Foote used the family plantation as the setting for the fictional Solitaire in his novel *Tournament*.

By Mike Jones' reckoning, the Law family story falls along similar lines. "The Laws have lived on the banks of Lake Washington since before the Civil War." The family and their descendants are buried a short pace down the road at Evergreen Cemetery. The approach to the cemetery is marked by the ruins of St. John's Episcopal Church. Built around 1830, St. John's Episcopal was one of the first churches in the region. During the Civil War, desperate soldiers melted down the lead frames around the stained-glass windows to make Confederate Minié balls. In 1907, the church took a direct hit from a tornado. A partial wall, the cornerstones, and a short portion of the belfry are the sole structural survivors.

The ruins of St. John's and the crumbling tombstones in Evergreen Cemetery bear witness to a complex settlement history along the lake, consisting of Native Americans, Africans, Civil War soldiers, and settlers rich and poor. "This is the heritage of the Delta. This represents who we are here in Washington County." Mike Jones views it all with profound sadness imbued with stubborn Southern pride.

Lagniappe: In the early morning hours of June 17, 2015, flames engulfed the once-magnificent Italianate mansion of Mt. Holly. It became a smoking skeleton. Only the blackened and scarred brick walls remained. The cause of the fire was reported to be "under investigation." Mike Jones' hopes to preserve this piece of Mississippi history were lost. The fate of the nearby Susie B. Law House remains perilous as it continues its slow trek to oblivion.

6

Voices from the Chamber

Voices from the past can convey a message, a thought, an emotion, or even a warning. At the Old Capitol Museum in Jackson, one dedicated spirit invested his entire life in trying to improve the health of his fellow citizens.

Following his death on January 9, 1959, Dr. Felix Underwood continued to earn accolades as "the man who saved a million lives." Underwood was born November 21, 1882, in Nettleton, a railroad town in Northeast Mississippi. At ten years of age, Felix watched helplessly as his mother died of infection following childbirth. Underwood made it his mission to revamp the public health practices of his day. Many believe that the good doctor's haunted footsteps in the corridors of the Old Capitol Museum are a sign he has not given up his quest.

The former state capitol building on South State Street is a survivor. From 1839 to 1903, this grand edifice hosted the Mississippi legislature. After sixty-four years of glorious service, it was abandoned when a new government building was erected to house the needs of a new era. In 1917, a group of ardent preservationists proposed restoring the structure and repurposing it for use by state agencies, including the board of health. In January of 1921, Felix Underwood, M.D., was appointed director of the Bureau of Child Hygiene and Welfare. The former country doctor became executive officer of the Mississippi State Board of Health in 1924, a position he held for the next thirty-four years.

Ruth Cole works as the daytime hostess for the Old Capitol Museum. Her personality is as cheerful and inviting as the floral-print, linen jacket she wears. She is happy to share her years of knowledge of the history of

The Old Capitol Museum in Jackson echoes with eerie sounds.

Dr. Underwood's portrait hangs in the Mississippi Hall of Fame.

the building and its occupants. She has high praise for Dr. Underwood. "Even after he retired, he was so dedicated that he'd come here to check on things on a volunteer basis. During that time, he had a heart attack while he was sitting at a desk and died."

Cole stands behind a large, half-moon-shaped welcome desk in the rotunda. To her immediate left, a museum security guard, in dark blue pants and shirt, sits and stares at a split-screen monitor. Cole leans over the glass counter and lowers her voice. "Some of our security police prefer not to be here at night. They think they hear somebody walking the halls when there is no one else in the building and nothing shows up on the security screens." One eyebrow arches sharply upward when it is suggested that the disembodied footsteps might belong to the deceased Dr. Underwood. "Well, he's the only one I know of to have actually died in the building."

Cole unfolds a brochure for a young couple just wandering in. The layout of the first floor is highlighted in blue. The two head off on their self-guided tour. Cole's smile is genuine as she watches them set out. "I'm never here at night. I'm lucky. When I hear footsteps, they all belong to real people."

Clay Williams is the museum's director. He is aware of the stories of the footsteps, along with another repetitive nocturnal sound. "I've had officers tell me that during the middle of the night, they hear kind of a thump coming from Dr. Underwood's old office on the first floor." At the time of Dr. Underwood's fatal heart attack, he fell forward and his head hit the top of the desk.

The museum takes a conservative stance when it comes to linking either the footsteps or the thumping sound to the good doctor. "We do get people who will ask if we have a ghost, and if they can do a paranormal investigation to prove who the ghost might be. The answer is no. The Mississippi Department of Archives and History would rather not be involved; we prefer that the emphasis be on the actual history."

Through the years, the paranormal sounds in the museum have struck a variety of chords. One incident involved Williams and his predecessor, Lucy Allen. "Back then, before Hurricane Katrina shut us down, I was in charge of exhibits. We were finishing up a temporary exhibit, and we were there pretty much every night to make the deadline," says Williams.

"Lucy was my director at the time. She was in her office and heard a bunch of banging around and assumed it was us."

Allen now serves as museum division director over all the state facilities. She summons up the basic facts of that evening. "Clay Williams, my head of the exhibits, and his assistant, John Gardner, had been working all day on the ground floor. My office is on the second floor. We close at five o'clock. A lot of times, I would stay after five. It was close to six, and I was ready to head out. When I opened my door, I heard them, or what I thought was them, continuing to work downstairs. My first thoughts were: 'My goodness, I am going to tell them that they need to go home. It's time we all go home and start over again tomorrow. They just need to take a break. They've been working way too hard.'"

Allen usually left the building by way of a back staircase leading to the parking lot. Due to her concerns about the staff, she chose to descend the grand staircase. "I wanted to be able to go past the exhibit room off the rotunda where they were working." Although she had just been listening to the distinct sounds of hammers and saws, "there was not anybody in the exhibit room," she said. "Not another soul in the building." Allen took a moment to assess the situation. "It did make me wonder why I was hearing as many noises as I was hearing, and how could that be?"

The next morning, Allen checked in with her staff. "I asked Clay and John, had they been staying late? Had they just gone out the door before I had? They said no. They had gone at the regular time—five o'clock; they were exhausted. They looked at me strangely and asked, 'Lucy, are you hearing things?' And I said, 'As a matter of fact, I am.'" Allen has a comfortable laugh, unafraid to appreciate the humor of the situation. "The sounds were very, very distinctive. It was definitely hammering and shuffling of things around on the floor. I heard that." The identity of the helpful poltergeists may never be known.

Allen also agrees that one of the most powerful exhibits in the museum does inadvertently evoke a sense of spirits returned from the dead. In the restored, second-floor Senate Chamber, wooden desks are set inside a ring of fluted columns. Ghostly, off-white, life-sized replicas of senators sit, stand, and gesture. A debate is in progress. The passage of the 1839 Married Woman's Property Act sparks a heated exchange. A cacophony of male voices echoes off the walls as advocates and opponents fight to have the final word: "Women are worthy of being queens." "This will sow discord and fraud." A spotlight shines down on each spectral figure as he makes his argument pro or con.

"One thing we wanted to do was bring history alive, rather than just show a stagnant room." Allen offers an explanation in defense of the eerie effect. "The monochromatic mannequins give you a flavor of the period, but at the same time, they do not depict a particular person, decade, or style of dress. The time period for the three debates you hear is from 1839 to 1903; that's when that chamber was used." Allen adds that the audio component, the "speaking statues," helps instill a greater sense of the hopes, expectations, and challenges facing these early leaders.

Prior to the final installation, the statues arrived "bagged and tagged."

The ghostly figures in the Senate Chamber.

It was a bizarre sight—humanlike forms encased in individual, clear, plastic shrouds. They reclined on their backs or sides; some had knees bent to be placed in chairs behind the desks. One anonymous staffer couldn't resist temptation. After unwrapping a standing statue, he positioned the "senator," with arm raised and finger outstretched, near one of the windows facing the street. Passersby would do a double take at the six-foot-tall specter, backlit by the lights inside the renovated Senate Chamber, as it stood in the window, gesturing down.

Clay Williams concurs. "I'm sure the sight of this all-white, humanlike form in the window at night spawned a host of stories that the museum is haunted."

Lucy Allen is unruffled at the prank. "There has to be some times when you have a little chuckle or fun with things . . . or it makes for some very long days."

Lagniappe: Built in 1839, the historic Old State Capitol building continues to undergo restoration and care. Yet, despite the intrusive sounds of repairs to the roof and interior spaces, whispers from the Senate Chamber still drift and wrap around the stately columns. The voices of those stalwart members opposed to the 1839 Married Woman's Property Act, or the 1861 secession from the Union, will not be quelled. History is not an illusion; it survives as a living entity passed from generation to generation. The Old Capitol Museum is merely the host, a place for figures from the past to gather and share the stories of who we are.

The Chapel of the Cross in Madison.

7

Madison's Chapel

North of the capital city of Jackson, in the rolling hills of Madison, a country chapel is forever haunted by a day that ended with the tragic death of the groom-to-be. A century and a half later, the ghost of the almost bride mourns at his gravesite.

The bride was the fair Helen, youngest daughter of John and Margaret Johnstone. Helen met her future fiancé, Henry Grey Vick, when his carriage broke down near Ingleside, her sister's stunning home. It was Christmas of 1857, and the dashing young man and the demure young lady fell immediately in love. At the insistence of Margaret, Helen's mother, Henry agreed to wait until Helen turned twenty before making her his wife. Henry courted Helen for two long years, traveling back and forth from Vicksburg to Madison County. At last, in the spring of 1859, wedding preparations were in progress. Helen and her sister Frances Britton helped their mother decorate the family's castlelike home, Annandale. The wedding ceremony would be held on the grounds of the Chapel of the Cross.

Local lore has it that during their courtship, Helen elicited one promise from her beloved: that he would never again use dueling as a means of settling a dispute. Four days before the wedding, Henry left for a trip to his family's ancestral home in Vicksburg and then on to New Orleans. While in the bustling port city, Henry ran into Laurence Washington Stith, a former classmate. Somewhere between the pleasantries and reminiscing, a perceived slight escalated into a full-blown accusation of sullying a man's honor. Dueling was illegal, so both men agreed to meet in secret at Bascomb Course in Mobile and resolve the issue facing them by drawing weapons.

There are two prevailing versions of what transpired during the duel.

The first is that Henry belatedly realized he was breaking his promise to Helen. To try to mitigate the circumstances, he kept to part of his vow: he would not kill. Henry shot his gun in the air and expected Laurence to do the same, thinking the two men would walk off the field together with their lives and honor intact.

C. M. Stanley, in an article for the *Alabama Journal,* holds with a different truth: Both men were lousy shots. Vick aimed for Stith's forehead. The bullet missed and struck a tree behind him; Stith aimed for Vick's body but shot him in the head instead.

Whatever the intent of the combatants, twenty-five-year-old Henry Grey Vick lay dead on the ground. Hours later, his body was placed on a steamer bound from New Orleans to Vicksburg. Also said to be on the steamer were a caterer with a crew of cooks and waiters, and food for the much anticipated wedding festivities to be held upriver at Annandale.

At Annandale, a servant announced that a courier on horseback was racing up the driveway. Mrs. Johnstone read the terse note: *Henry Vick killed today. Duel in Mobile.* Helen screamed and fell to the floor. The wedding decorations were hastily pulled down and funeral preparations begun. At midnight, May 20, 1859, mourners gathered. Men were stationed with torches to light the long driveway leading up to the Chapel of the Cross. Digging commenced for a grave for the groom in the cemetery behind the rear altar of the chapel. Helen was said to have worn her wedding gown to the service. She cut off locks of her hair and these were placed over the heart of the fallen groom-to-be.

Helen swore she would never marry another. A tombstone, made to resemble the crossed limbs of a hewn tree trunk, was erected at the head of Henry's grave. Helen had an iron bench installed next to it. Here she sat day after day, month after month, pinning for her lost love.

Three years later, Helen's resolved weakened. In August of 1862, she married Dr. George C. Harris, a Confederate chaplain, who went on to serve as clergyman at the Chapel of the Cross. The couple lived at Mt. Helena, a grand home in Sharkey County. Helen Johnstone Harris died a widow in 1917, six years after her husband. By all accounts it was a happy marriage, yet Helen never forgot her first true love. In her final moments, she believed she was a young bride again about to walk down the aisle; she died peacefully with a vision of Henry waiting for her.

On balmy spring nights, the "Bride of Annandale" returns to the Chapel of the Cross. Light from the full moon catches in the folds of Helen's wedding gown as she steps lightly through the cemetery and sits on the bench next to Henry's grave.

Ruth Cole works at the Old Capitol Museum in Jackson, and is a life-long resident of the area. "I am a member of the Children of the American Revolution, and as part of service to the community, we'd help out at historic sites." Cole remembers excursions to the Chapel of the Cross. "This was a time when that area of the county was not as developed as it was now; it was very, very, rural. The setting itself, the woods was a bit spooky. The Chapel was only open once a month on Sundays. We'd go there to help with the cleaning. We'd sweep and dust." Cole says that as a child, she had heard the stories of Henry and Helen, and that Helen's ghost returned sometimes to the cemetery. "It was all a bit eerie."

Lagniappe: The formal entrance to the cemetery is to the immediate right of the chapel. A pair of massive iron gates is inscribed with the family name: *Johnstone*. The gates are an intricate design of intertwined branches and leaves. Henry Vick's grave and Helen's bench are underneath the arched chapel windows. Scattered throughout the rural cemetery are other carved headstones and statuary. Most touching are the tributes by grieving parents for children lost in infancy. One headstone is capped with a stone pillow. Tassels hang from the four corners. In bas-relief, two little girls, one appearing slightly younger and smaller than the other, lie on their sides. The tiny replicas face each other, knees slightly bent. The inscription on the base of the tomb gives only their first names: *Anna* and *Helen*. One sweet tale says that the spirits of two little girls are occasionally seen playing and swinging on the cemetery gates.

Debbie Rayner, a tall, thin, pale blond, is a member of the Altar Guild at the Chapel of the Cross. She says she is unaware of who the ghost children might be who play near the gates. Spectral visitors don't bother her; the intruders she wishes would just find another home are of the furry variety. After the morning service, she helps to pull a large sheet of plastic over the altar. "We have flying squirrels that leave droppings; they squeeze inside through holes near the rafters." Rayner also has a problem with a few of the more lurid tales associated with the historic

The headstone of Helen and Anna.

chapel. "This is still an active Episcopal church. There was an article in the *Northside Sun*, our local paper, and it talked about blood appearing on the floor like this was a crime scene. It bothered me. It's the opposite of how we feel about this place. More than anything, for most of us in the congregation, it is very peaceful here."

As a precaution, at dusk, the gates at the bottom of the hill, leading to the chapel and the cemetery, are locked. Visitors real or imagined are not encouraged after hours.

8

Rowan Oak

*It is my ambition to be as private a person as possible, abolished and
voided from history . . . that the sum and history of my life, which in the
same sentence is my obit and epitaph too, shall be both:
He made the books and he died.*
—William Faulkner

A peculiar genius, Nobel Prize-winning author William Cuthbert
Faulkner reveled in a good ghost story. Hunkered down at Rowan Oak,
his home and retreat on the outskirts of Oxford, Mississippi, he wrote
about the darker side of human emotions in nineteen acclaimed adult
novels and eighty short stories. He saved the tale of his favorite ghost for
the children. She was the beautiful Judith Sheegog.

Faulkner delighted in repeating the supernatural yarn of a tragic spirit
who haunted the gardens. "The one interesting thing about Faulkner's
favorite ghost is that he never wrote the story down, so I've heard five
or six different versions," says William Griffith, the curator of Rowan
Oak. "One version is that the daughter of the original owner, Col. Robert
Sheegog, fell in love with two soldiers and couldn't decide which one to
marry. They killed each other in a duel, and Judith threw herself off the
balcony because there would be no one to court her anymore. Another
twist on the tale is that Judith was killed by a stray bullet when the two
soldiers fought over her." A sly smile slips out as the curator delivers version number three. "One was a Confederate soldier, the other was Union.
He was the one Judith really loved, and when he was killed in battle, she
threw herself off the balcony." And for a final bit of drama, there is option

Rowan Oak deep in Bailey's Woods.

number four. Judith was climbing down a rope ladder, tied to the balcony, to elope with her beloved Union soldier. She slipped and fell to her death.

Drew Chiles is a history student pursuing a master's degree at the University of Mississippi. He works as a part-time guide at Rowan Oak. Chiles is familiar with the saga of Judith Sheegog. "She had been unlucky in love, flung herself off the balcony, and her body is buried underneath the magnolia tree."

Griffith settles into a worn armchair in a back hallway of Rowan Oak. "They are all great stories with one common denominator—Judith dies in every one. She ends up buried in the garden in the front of the house and the garden is haunted." The curator's thin frame is nearly lost among the oversized chair cushions. Dressed in a rumpled white shirt and slacks, he is every inch the distracted scholar focused on facts, not fashion. "Faulkner may have created the different versions himself. At Halloween, he was known to tell the story with props, rattling chains . . . and another time he enlisted Cho-Cho, his eldest stepdaughter. While the other children were asleep, he had Cho-Cho slip downstairs and start playing the piano. Faulkner got the other kids up by telling them, 'Oh, the piano is playing by itself.' Of course, Cho-Cho ran and hid." Griffith realigns himself in the chair. "Faulkner loved ghost stories. Who doesn't? Especially in a house like this, you'd expect it to be haunted, have a ghost. You'd want it to have a ghost."

Faulkner certainly agreed, and he had an ulterior motive for keeping Judith's restless spirit alive. When he purchased the home in 1930, it was known simply as the old Bailey Place. The dense forest that surrounded the Greek Revival home was called Bailey's Woods. "It was pretty run down; the house had been abandoned for about seven years, and the pastures were rented out to a farmer who kept his herds on the grounds," says Griffith.

Faulkner was immediately enamored with the Gothic state of disrepair. While he updated the electricity and the plumbing inside the house, and later added an addition to the back, he wanted the gardens left as overgrown ruins. He concurred completely with second owner Grace

Judith's burial site in Rowan Oak's garden.

Bailey, who called the entire grounds "a vulgar formality."

Estelle, Faulkner's wife, disagreed. She especially wanted to restore Colonel Sheegog's antebellum maze garden in the front of the house. A circle of cedars ringed the perimeter. Inside the maze, concentric circles of raised brick beds contained sweet shrub and privet hedges. A magnolia tree grew in the center. During the Reconstruction era, and later by Grace Bailey's strict edict, the maze garden was left untended. "She just let the landscaping go. Volunteer trees—we call them that because they are self-seeding—grew up between the bricks and their heavy shade wiped out the hedges." Griffith says that Estelle argued with her husband and even tried to enlist the support of her children to restore the garden to its original splendor. Faulkner argued back that "only new money would ruin that garden." To ensure that nothing in the garden would ever be disturbed, Faulkner resurrected the ghost of Judith. "He said that if anyone messes with Judith's garden, where she is buried, it will anger her spirit. She'll come to haunt the house instead of the garden," states Griffith.

Faulkner won. Today, towering magnolia trees dominate the space. Widespread branches, lush with iridescent green leaves and fragrant blossoms, cover the red bricks. "We maintain it the way Faulkner liked it, not as Colonel Sheggog and his family had it." Griffith admits, that just like Estelle, some contemporary visitors also object. "Yes, to the surprise, shock, and sometimes horror of many garden club members, we have not brought it back to the 1840s. We keep the property as Faulkner had . . . and that's all we'll ever do."

Rowan Oak was donated to the University of Mississippi by Faulkner's daughter, Jill, with the understanding that it remain as it was when her father was alive. The Do-Not-Disturb policy also guarantees that the alleged burial spot of the ghost of Judith Sheegog will remain untouched.

Faulkner lived on the property for two years before he gave it a name. "Faulkner loved legends. He was greatly influenced by Sir James Frazer's *Golden Bough*, a giant twelve-volume series about Celtic folklore, so he called his home Rowan Oak for the rowan tree of Scotland and the oak tree of America." According to Celtic legend, the boughs of the rowan tree, when placed over a doorway, ward off evil spirits. "It was kind of a joke and it kind of wasn't a joke," explains Griffith. "Faulkner's evil spirits were the tax man and the media. He felt compelled to have his estate have a name because of Southern tradition, and he also took those traditions and put his own spin on them."

Inside Rowan Oak today, Faulkner's personal belongings are scattered about as if the writer has just moved on to the next room. His glasses rest on a pile of books in the library; his favorite pair of riding boots are standing by a chair; neckties are flung over a dresser mirror in the bedroom; a pipe and cans of tobacco await the owner in his study; and the upper third of the walls bear the large script of his handwritten outline for a novel. Student guide Chiles says that it's the little things that cause some to believe in Faulkner's abiding presence. "People that have worked here say that they would walk into a room and it would smell like pipe smoke." Chiles, a tall, young man with curly, light brown, shoulder-length hair, expresses disappointment tinged with hope. "I haven't seen anything, but I'm waiting. I am looking forward to it. I'd love to see his ghost writing on the walls the way some have reported."

"I'm not against people who do believe that William Faulkner is still here.

Faulkner's glasses where he left them in the front parlor.

Faulkner's bedroom with his riding boots and pants hung over the chair.

The study where William Faulkner liked to write on the walls.

That would be just too good to be true," says Griffith, suppressing a grin. "But if we do have a ghost, it's not him. [Every] once in awhile we'll get psychics, and if what they are saying is believable, what they describe to me sounds more like Colonel Sheegog than William Faulkner."

In an upstairs bedroom, psychics report sighting a spirit dressed in a dark frock coat and top hat. "They say the old gentleman keeps asking why he has so much company coming into his house, and the spirit complains to the psychics that he doesn't have enough staff to accommodate them all." Griffith adds that the curator before him would say he did hear unusual sounds, eerie enough to make the surroundings feel uncomfortable. With a slight dash of cynicism, Griffith says, "Sure, I'm uncomfortable too when I am here by myself at night. Who wouldn't be? It's pitch black out here. No street lights make it back this far. The only illumination outside is the single bulb in the porch light . . . but nothing has ever happened to me."

Griffith rethinks his statement. His eyes are drawn to a revolving rack in the corner. Its shelves are crammed with magazines, newspaper articles, and one mysterious photograph. He gets up, digs through a pile, and returns to show off an eight-by-ten glossy. "It's a weird photo," he begins. "When I first took over as curator, there was a lot of renovation, a bunch of work needed to be done. Once we got funding, we stood in the center of each room and took photographs in order for us to put the furniture back in the right spots."

The photo Griffith holds is an enlargement of Estelle's room. Faulkner had the room, with its light-filled windows, added for his wife to use as both bedroom and painting studio. There is an easel set-up in the corner near the bed. Griffith directs the attention to the north window in the photo. "I didn't notice this at first, but my assistant did. Look through the three panes on the bottom. In the center pane, you can see someone sitting on a bench. In the pane to the right, you see a little cherry tree, and there is a child or a woman standing next to it." Griffith grasps the photo with both hands and gives it a little shake. "If you go up to Estelle's bedroom right now, you can look through that window; you'll clearly see a grape arbor and behind that a house, the old servant's quarters." He holds the photo up for inspection. "This photograph was taken in January, wintertime. No big, leafy trees to block the view. In the photo, the house and the grape arbor are gone. Where they should be is a black void, negative space.

In the foreground, we have a woman on a bench and another woman or child to the right as if they are conversing." On the day the photo was taken there were no visitors allowed on the grounds "What is so shocking about this is that it is a documentary photograph for the purpose of expediting a move. We did not take it to try and capture a ghost or prove anything other than the location of the furniture."

Mammy Callie's house is the wooden structure that has vanished in the photograph. Visitors to Rowan Oak can go to the backyard and still see the house Faulkner built for his beloved family caretaker, Caroline Barr, better known to all as "Mammy Callie." Mammy Callie lived there from 1930 to 1940. "Faulkner brought her to Rowan Oak when she was around ninety years old. She had been his nanny, but she didn't come here to retire. She took care of his two stepchildren and his daughter, Jill," says Griffith. Faulkner never knew his nanny's exact age. Mammy Callie remembered being in her mid-teens when the Civil War broke out and around twenty when it ended. She cared for Faulkner's children until the day she died from a stroke. Faulkner held her funeral service in the front parlor. She is buried in the African American section of the cemetery. The epitaph on her grave reads *"Mammy Callie. Her white children bless her."*

When asked to speculate if the figure on the bench in the photograph might be Mammy Callie, Griffith replies candidly, "I would love it. It wouldn't surprise me if it turned out to be her because she was very dedicated to the family. She really was very much part of the Faulkner family lore and affections."

As for the other phantom figures standing near the cherry tree, theories are all over the place. Colonel Sheegog's wife? Faulkner's wife? The cantankerous Grace Bailey? Could the second figure in the photo be that of a child? Faulkner's first daughter, Alabama, only lived nine days and is buried in the Faulkner family plot at St. Peter's, so she would seem unlikely. Faulkner's second daughter, Jill, lived to be a healthy adult. Naturally, the speculation veers toward Faulkner's beautiful ghost, the haunted Judith Sheegog. On the day the photo was taken, was she restless enough to venture from her burial place beneath the magnolia tree and join another group of spirits near the grape arbor? It would be a lovely thing, indeed.

Mammy Callie's house on the grounds.

Lagniappe: A cemetery and a statue. On finishing his final novel about the inhabitants of the fictional Yoknapatawpha County, Faulkner said he was done. He had "broken the pencil," and wasn't going to write any more. "He wanted to buy this big estate in Virginia, teach at the University of Virginia, and spend the rest of his years with his daughter and his grandchildren." Rowan Oak curator William Griffith says that although Faulkner was ill, his death in 1962 "shocked everyone."

"He was sixty-four, fell off his horse, and injured himself more severely than he realized. He resorted to his usual whiskey therapy, which is how he often dealt with injuries, heartache, or disappointment. He'd go to his room, go on a binge, and wait for it to pass. This time it was taking too long; he'd been lying in bed a couple of weeks, drinking very heavily, eating very little, and he asked Estelle to 'take me to the clinic in Byhalia.'" Estelle complied. However, according to Griffith, "As soon as the family left, he had a heart attack and died."

Faulkner often expressed a desire to be buried at Rowan Oak, but he never put his wishes in writing. "Estelle buried him at St. Peter's Cemetery in Oxford, and later she was buried next to him." Their side-by-side stone slabs are etched with names and dates. On her husband's, Estelle had inscribed *"Beloved Go With God."*

In lieu of flowers, there are occasional tributes from those who come to bring sustenance for Faulkner's spirit. On one dreary, wet, summer afternoon, it's an amber-colored bottle of beer. "He preferred whiskey," says Griffith, "but they'll leave a bottle of bourbon too." When quizzed about his basic requirements, Faulkner wrote, "The tools I need for my trade are paper, tobacco, food, and a little whiskey."

Griffith corrects one misconception about the famed novelist's drinking habits. "He didn't drink to write; he needed it to let go. He had a hard time letting go." A prodigious drinker, Faulkner had rules when it came to imbibing. Griffith ticks them off, "You shouldn't drink beer after sunset, that's tacky. Vodka, scotch, bourbon, and whiskey are inside

William and Estelle Faulkner's graves in St. Peter's Cemetery.

drinks, and gin is an outside drink. Mint juleps are served in a metal cup; no other kind of cup will do."

The town of Oxford prefers to honor longtime resident William Faulkner with pipe, not drink in hand. In the historic Oxford Courthouse Square, a bronze statue of Faulkner sits on a bench in front of

Faulkner's controversial statue in front of Oxford's City Hall.

the red-brick Romanesque Revival Oxford City Hall. When the statue was dedicated in 1997, on the centennial of Faulkner's birth, family and some friends objected, saying they didn't get it right either. "Faulkner made it very clear how he felt about statues; he was against them," states Griffith. "The family felt it was a tasteless gesture. . . . He never would have sat on a public bench in a welcoming posture for you to sit next to him." In one newspaper article, his brother, Chooky Faulkner, wondered, "What effect a stick of dynamite might have on it?" A nephew was unhappy with having his uncle being reduced to a tourist attraction.

A *Saturday Evening Post* article quotes the author on his wishes for life after death: "If I was reincarnated, I'd want to come back as buzzard. Nothing hates him or envies him or wants him or needs him. He's never bothered or in danger."

9

The King Lives On in Tupelo

They arrive by plane, tour bus, RV, car, and motorcycle caravan. Decades after his death, they come not to mourn but to connect. For these diehard fans, there is no question that Elvis's spirit lingers near his childhood home in Tupelo, Mississippi. "We have an elderly woman who visits four or five times a week," says Dick Guyton, former executive director of the Elvis Presley Memorial Foundation. "She sits on the front porch on that swing right there and talks to Elvis. She moved from Florida to Tupelo to be closer to him." Guyton, a tall man, wearing a green museum polo shirt and khaki slacks, hesitates before revealing more. "At first, we thought she might be a distraction to other visitors. She has these animated conversations as if she can hear him. We don't know what she sees; she's never described her vision. This obviously means so much to her, so now we just let her be."

The fifteen-acre Elvis Presley Birthplace and Museum complex draws both the curious and the loyal. Local resident Lisa Hall is amazed. "People turn up in Tupelo from all over Europe and the United States. Two ladies—one's from Montana and one is from Idaho—they meet here every year to be near Elvis." Not all claim to see his ghost, but the experience of walking in Elvis's footsteps is often overwhelming.

Sybil Presley Clark is a distant cousin. She keeps vigil perched on a stool just inside the door of the two-room, shotgun-style cottage where the young Elvis lived. As the hostess assigned to the birthplace, Clark has dealt with a wide range of reactions. "There was an Elvis impersonator from Brazil here the other day." Guyton interjects; he prefers the term "Elvis tribute artist." An exuberant Clark shakes her streaked, steel-gray-

Elvis Presley's birthplace in Tupelo.

and-white hair and continues as if there has been no interruption. "In walks this tall, beautiful, young man, a big artist in Brazil, and as soon as he steps in the room, he can't even talk. He's just crying, tears rolling down." The Brazilian artist's emotional outburst preceded Clark's poignant recitation of the King of Rock 'n' Roll's first moments.

"Elvis was born right here." Clark waves her hand over the handmade quilt covering the iron bed that is set on a diagonal to the fireplace. "Of course, you all know he had a stillborn twin, and because of that, Gladys became the overprotective mommy. Elvis slept with her all his little life. There used to be a crib. They took it out because he didn't sleep there; he slept in his mother's arms. When he started school, she would walk him back and forth. The other children teased him and called him a momma's boy." Clark pauses to give the group, crowded into the small bedroom, time to absorb the details. She has grown accustomed to the fans' deep attachment to Elvis, but it's taken a little time.

The bed where Elvis was born.

This Presley cousin listens with polite Southern restraint while visitors regale her with tales of ghostly encounters. "Just the other day, it was so precious; some girls, who go to a church in Ohio, said that their pastor got in an elevator with Elvis. The pastor started to witness to Elvis, and Elvis stopped him and said, 'I gave my life to Christ when I was twelve years old.'"

Guyton is pleased that fans like to share their stories and remembrances, yet he is not fully on the ghostly bandwagon. "We'll joke about going into the house in the morning, and the picture in the bedroom will be crooked on the wall, and the staff will say, 'Well, Elvis must have been here.'"

Clark says she doesn't need ghost tales to be reminded of him. She pats the *I-Miss-Elvis* button over her heart. "Being here every day, I do feel close to him. I was raised with Elvis. He was eight years older than me." Clark looks out the single window on to the street. "Within three blocks around here, this place could have been called Presleyville. Elvis's grandfather and my grandfather Noah were brothers. There were ten of those kids. My grandfather Noah raised his family on First Street and had seventeen kids. Elvis was just one of many, many cousins." She smiles and her blue eyes light up behind wire-framed glasses. "We didn't know he was going to be famous. My older sister was his buddy, and I was the pesky little sister, so he has always been part of my life."

And for a couple from Saranac Lake in upstate New York, Elvis will always be a part of their life together. Making a pilgrimage to his birthplace, they are convinced that the young Elvis has returned to Tupelo. Filled with nervous anticipation, Randy and Holly Miner are taking pictures of the 450-square-foot, white clapboard home at its original location on the southwest corner of the property.

"This was a surprise for me," proclaims a wide-eyed Holly. "Our anniversary is the twenty-sixth of August, and we've traveled over 4,100 miles to be here. My husband didn't tell me where we were going to celebrate our thirty-third anniversary."

"Elvis died ten days before our wedding," Randy Miner announces as he stands stiffly beside his wife. "We got married August 26, 1977."

"I always wanted to come see him, and ten days before we were married, he passed away, and I was like, I will never get to see him." Holly crosses her hands over her chest and rubs her arms up and down. "It gives me goosebumps to be here. I've got chills. This is where Elvis started off, and now I get to be with him where he was at the beginning."

Guyton does not find it at all unusual that a couple would link their wedding anniversary with Elvis's death. "Everyone knows where they were and what they were doing when JFK was assassinated, and Elvis fans around the world remember where they were and what they were doing when he died on August 16, 1977."

After his phenomenal rise to fame, Elvis built a grand mansion in Memphis and lived a lifestyle far removed from his humble beginnings in Tupelo. To Dick Guyton, this has little bearing on the true nature of the man whose music took on an iconic status. "Elvis came back to Tupelo a lot; he never forgot where he came from. He would drive down from Memphis in the evening and spend two, three, four hours visiting." To avid fans, this is proof enough that Elvis's heart and soul remain in Tupelo, not at his Graceland mansion.

Cousin Clark also emphasizes Elvis's strong ties to his birthplace. "Elvis's father, Vernon; his uncle; and his grandfather Jessie Presley built this house in 1934." Clark points to one of the rare photographs of the child Elvis with his parents. Father Vernon and mother Gladys appear uncomfortable, yet their impish three-year-old exhibits no such qualms. The young Puck wears a scaled-down fedora-style hat, cocked sideways. His cherubic cheeks and full lips hint at drama ahead. Not long after the photo was taken in 1937, the Presleys lost their home when Vernon went to prison for altering the figures on a check he received for payment on a hog.

Sybil Clark remains indignant about the severity of the punishment, and she is pleased to be able to announce with a well-satisfied smile, "Twenty years later, Elvis comes back here famous, and he bought the house and took it back. Then, he built a swimming pool and a ballpark and installed playground equipment for the community. He did it for the children, built a beautiful park so they could have what he never did."

Once the park was built, Elvis had a dream, a premonition of sorts. Dick Guyton, his voice in the lower register, explains what happened. "Not too many years before he died, Elvis and Janelle McComb, a dear friend of his from Tupelo, were walking the property and reminiscing. Elvis turned to Janelle and said, 'You know, it would be nice to have a sort of meditation place out here.' The story is that he used to go to the overlook on the backside of our property, take his guitar, sit, and look out over the lights of Tupelo."

When Elvis died, his fans were devastated. As the news of his passing spread, "fan clubs from everywhere sent money for no reason," according to Guyton, "and the city fathers said, 'What are we going to do with this money?' And Janelle stepped forward and said, 'Elvis wanted a meditation place; why can't we build a chapel?' That's how it started."

The Elvis Presley Memorial Chapel is a contemporary design. "The chapel was dedicated in 1979, two years after he died. I think he would have approved," says Guyton as his eyes sweep the interior. "We play Elvis gospel music. And you walk in here and there will be someone sitting quietly, listening to the music, saying a prayer, tears in their eyes. We have a few local people who visit regularly and spend twenty to thirty minutes. Yeah, this is where they feel closest to him."

A woman in her late fifties gets up from one of the oak pews. She has been staring at a bank of five stained-glass windows that line the front wall. The brilliant purples, greens, lavenders, golds, and blues are arranged in a semiabstract mosaic pattern. The visitor adjusts her glasses and approaches the center panel. "I see him," she exclaims with delight. "There's his face and his arms are stretched up to the heavens." Elvis sightings in the chapel are a fairly common occurrence, says Guyton. "Once one person sees the pattern in the glass, then everybody crowds around looking for more."

Other fans arrive with tokens of their love and respect. Pedestals are provided for the daily flow of fresh flowers: a dozen yellow roses, a spray of mums, a single red rose. It is a perpetual wake inside the chapel. The mourners share a common bond: they are unwilling to let go of their memories. Guyton knows why. "Even if they didn't know him, never saw him perform, if they came from the same kind of poor background, they can relate. The birthplace is all about the little boy. . . . These were

Elvis sightings are common in the chapel's stained-glass windows.

the formative years that affected the rest of his life, so the fans by coming here, they can connect. His family didn't have anything, and yet, Elvis rose to be the greatest entertainer of all times. The gospel music that he sang in the church, music that he heard in Shake Rag, the Black section of town, and the mixture of his music that made his a totally different sound, all came from his roots here in Tupelo."

In addition to the chapel, there is another house of worship on the grounds. The Assembly of God Church is where the Presleys attended services on Sunday mornings and Wednesday evenings. Visitors are ushered inside the actual wooden, one-room structure. A hush descends. All eyes are on the pulpit. The austere podium matches the stark simplicity of the country church. As if on angels' wings, three white screens silently descend from narrow slits in the paneled ceiling. During the multimedia presentation, the former congregation appears dressed in their humble 1940s-era Sunday best. Brother Frank Smith steps up to the pulpit and the spirit-filled service commences. There is a call to renounce evil, a laying on of hands for the fallen and repentant, and enough gospel music to cause hips to sway and hands to clap. Brother Smith calls upon the young Presley family to step forward. With eyes lowered, ten-year-old Elvis quietly begins to sing, "Jesus Loves Me," and the new congregation of twenty-first-century visitors join in. Many are so caught up in the fifteen-minute presentation that they forget it is all a reenactment, caught on tape and rewound for their benefit.

If all of this is not enough to evoke the spirit of Elvis, there is more—an opportunity to hold his hand. In the center of the complex, between his childhood home and the Assembly of God church, thirteen-year-old Elvis waits impatiently. He is caught midstride. His oversized, hand-me-down coveralls bunch around his ankles. A guitar, purchased by his mother from the Tupelo Hardware store, dangles from his left hand. But it is his right hand that is a fan magnet. Avid devotees squeeze in for a photo op. They nestle their heads low on his shoulder. Then, trance-like, they slip their fingers into his right hand, curled ever so slightly upward. The physical contact, albeit with a bronze statue, elicits sighs, smiles—pure joy. "We have sixty to sixty-five thousand people a year—almost seven hundred thousand people have touched that statue," boasts Guyton.

The statue of Elvis as a young boy is a big draw.

From the elderly woman who moved to Tupelo to commune daily with Elvis, to the couple who track their wedding anniversary by aligning it with Elvis's untimely demise, to those who sit in the chapel and are moved to tears, finding Elvis in Tupelo is a spiritual journey. Here they have faith that the young, innocent Elvis Aaron Presley hovers close by.

Lagniappe: The centerpiece of the Elvis Presley Birthplace is the museum. Through exhibits and audio-video presentations, visitors see firsthand the effects of the Great Depression. There are family photos of Elvis's maternal grandparents, aunts, uncles, and cousins. Gospel music, ballads, and the folk tunes of the era play softly. Every artifact bears witnesses to the theme: "We all know it ended. This is how it began." Much of the original collection came from Janelle McComb, who met Elvis as a two-year-old in Tupelo. She later became his number-one fan and often acted as a second mother following the death of Gladys Presley. Janelle saved everything.

Guyton points to a small glass case—a treasure chest of toys, including marbles, kites, and comic books. "Elvis loved comic books. His favorite character was Captain Marvel, who had a bolt of lightning on his costume." Guyton believes the design heavily influenced Elvis throughout his career. "If you'll notice Elvis's hair, it always hung in a point down his forehead. It's quite the same shape. His jewelry, the TCB [Taking Care of Business] necklace, has a bolt of lightning."

One blue velvet costume brings a flood of memories to the museum's former director. "Elvis was four years older than me, and I was sixteen when he performed a benefit concert at the fairgrounds for the city of Tupelo. Town boy makes it big," says Guyton with evident pride. "Everybody celebrated. It was so hot; it was in early September 1957. Elvis had on that blue velvet shirt, and he was burning up, and we were burning up."

The weirdest exhibit displays bedlinens and towels from a motel room where the King stayed during a concert in Monroe, Louisiana. "Two ladies went in and collected everything he touched, including those two coffee cups and a wet towel. One of the ladies put the towel in her freezer for a number of years, and after Janelle opened the museum, she gave it to her, as well as the coffee cup, which still has coffee in it." The rarest item is as personal as it gets. "If you look real close, there is a piece of scotch tape over a black hair on that towel."

Guyton repeats that the museum owes its existence to Janelle Mc-Comb. "Janelle often wrote the cards for the family—birthday cards and holiday cards for Lisa Marie and her dad. Vernon commissioned her to write the epitaph for Elvis's grave."

The epitaph reads in part, "He became a living legend in his own time; earning the respect and love of millions." Above the tombstone is an eternal flame erected by McComb and nine other close friends and associates. On the base is a telling inscription, also penned by McComb: *May this flame . . . serve as a constant reminder to each of us of your eternal presence.*

10

Tupelo's Lyric Theatre

His name is Antoine. He has been haunting Tupelo's Lyric Theatre for as long as anyone can remember. His past is murky, but his activities in the present day keep the staff in turmoil. Lisa Hall is the theatre's box office manager. Fringes of short dark hair frame her startling, near-turquoise-blue eyes. Wearing a bright-yellow blouse, Hall looks like an effervescent pixie who has just flown in from the shores of Neverland. Instead, her command post is the front desk and her archenemy is not Captain Hook, but the mysterious Antoine, a ghost with a penchant for mischief. Hall recounts a typical incident. "We were upstairs in the costume room, and we had moved some things around, and we left. We came back a little later and everything had been rearranged, and there was no one in the building but us."

Tracie Maxey-Conwill serves on the board of directors of the community theatre. Maxey-Conwill is a statuesque blond dressed in a simple white blouse and black pencil skirt. "I never had any problems with Antoine until our annual Fall Haunted House." As an all-volunteer operation, the Lyric Theatre Board relies on revenue from memberships, ticket sales, corporate sponsors, and an annual Halloween Haunted House fundraiser. Each year, members pitch in to transform the stately old theatre into a spook-filled, monster mansion.

Maxey-Conwill describes the huge undertaking and how one disgruntled ghost went for his own special effects. "We had hung large sheets of black plastic upstairs on every wall of the back hallway so all of our light switches were covered. We just put blue lights in, and we left those on 24/7 while we got ready for haunted theatre. We had cleared

The haunted theatre in downtown Tupelo.

out everybody, and I was going back through checking on everything. I was at the corner, near the bathroom, and all the blue lights went off." Maxey-Conwill lets out an exasperated sigh. "I knew no one could get to the light switches, or would know where they were, so I had to assume it was him [Antoine], and I said, 'I have never messed with you. Do not mess with me.' Just as I gave him his marching orders, the lights popped back on. The next thing I remember was that I was in the lobby, and I don't know how I got there."

Executive director Tom Booth is standing in the office listening to Maxey-Conwill. He cocks his head to the side, surprised at her revelation. "I never heard about this. When was this?"

"That was two years ago."

Booth glances from Maxey-Conwill to Hall, inhales slowly, and then in a powerful, deep undertone decides to share. "I've had two haunted experiences, both late at night. We had an event here; I had left the

stage area, closed everything down, came back, and came in this door."
Booth indicates the entrance to the office to the right of the main lobby
doors. "When I came in the door, I heard, I can only describe it as sort
of laughing/singing, *"La La La. Ha Ha Ha Ha Ha."* And I replied back,
sarcastically, 'Ha Ha. Very funny.' Being a volunteer organization, there
is always a director, a production manager. A lot of people have keys.
People come in at all hours. So when I heard the voice, I thought there
must be somebody in the building; they heard me drive up late at night
and were trying to scare me. I go throughout the entire building, upstairs, out the stage door, all the way around the outside. Of course, the
place is empty. There is nobody here." Booth rolls his pale-blue eyes. "I
got my keys and I went home. It was very creepy."

Booth shifts his stance. A black Lyric Theatre T-shirt molds to his well-
toned upper body. Part two of his inexplicable encounters unfolds. "The
other time, it was late at night. I came in my office door. We had had a
party, a dinner with beautiful flower arrangements. They were just going
to go to waste, so I was going to get them and carry them to my church
so they could be used the next day." Booth folds his arms across his chest.
"I got them. I loaded them in my car. I came back in and realized that
some lights had been left on. I go through the building cutting out lights,
checking air conditioning, and I get ready to go." Booth hesitates, pats
his pockets, and looks around, imitating his actions of that night. "I can't
find my keys." His voice takes on a puzzled air. "I backtrack all my steps,
go out to my car, search everywhere, [and] search the building; thirty or
forty-five minutes later I give up." Booth throws two muscular arms in the
air. "I go to the phone to call someone to come get me." As a theatre director, Booth slips easily into the role of actor and demonstrates. He steps
over to the inside wall lined end to end with a narrow counter. It serves as
desk and catchall for a myriad of office equipment: fax machine, printer,
stacks of paperwork, and a black phone resting on a clear Plexiglas stand.
The stand has a slot to the right to hold pencils and paper clips.

All eyes are on Booth as he continues with his recreation. "I start to
punch in numbers on the phone and I look down in this slot and there
are my keys, wedged in there tight." Booth stares at his audience and in
a firm voice announces, "I have never put my keys in there. I would have
no reason to put my keys there."

The issue of how his errant keys were jammed into the unlikely location still gnaws at him. "I spent about half the next week trying to bounce my keys in there and couldn't do it." His irritation is apparent. If the culprit is the illusive Antoine, Booth has no explanation for how the ghost pulled it off or even why. "I have tried to figure out some logic to it all. Once again, all I could do at the time was yank out my keys, lock the doors, and go home."

One theatre volunteer believes she has a photo of the ghost. "There's a lady here that works for the Haunted House Theatre event we do here every year, and she has this picture and she swears it is Antoine." Hall has seen it, but she's skeptical. "She showed it to us; there is a white shadow and these lights go out from it. I think it is just something that happened in the processing of the picture, but she really believes she caught him on camera."

What bothers office manager Lisa Hall more are the noises and the odors. She tries to justify it all and fails. "Now the slamming of doors could just be part of the old building and drafts, and the traces of smoke— we have a No Smoking policy here—so I guess that odor could be left over from before, but sometimes the smoke smell is awfully strong. And sometimes you hear shuffling coming from the stage area when no one is there." Hall leans in, her voice a whisper, and states, "There was a girl who came in from a nearby town. . . . She wanted to do one of those paranormal investigations, and I told her I couldn't give permission. I would have to check with our board and let her know. As soon as she left—there was nobody here but me and Claire who also works here— this door behind me that leads into the theater space slammed shut so hard it was like Antoine didn't want her here." Hall glances quickly over her shoulder as if fearful the ghost might hear her talking about him. "If Claire had not been here, I would have thought it was just the wind, but all the doors were closed." Hall adds that Claire will not go upstairs by herself. She refuses to enter the second-floor costume, prop, and dressing rooms without accompaniment.

Booth shrugs it off. "I've spent the night in the theatre, maybe three, four, five times through the years, working very late. It would be one, two, or three o'clock in the morning. I'd be just wiped out. I live thirty minutes from here. I'd find a couch or a bed on the set, go upstairs, get a blanket or a pillow out of our prop room, and go to sleep. Never heard a thing." He corrects himself. "Well, I shouldn't say never heard a thing. The floors pop. This is like an old building, over one hundred years."

Booth's nonchalant attitude gets a jolt. "Look at that!" A thick drop of water plops down from the center of the ceiling and makes a loud splat on the floor. The director goes for the punch line: "Looks like Antoine just spit at us." There is nervous laughter from the rest of the group in the room. "It's like if we leave and then come back in, we disturb him, and it annoys him."

Hall agrees. "People are convinced that as long as you leave him alone, he is not mean, except to slam the door to express his displeasure."

Why does this ghost prefer solitude over company, and where did the name Antoine come from? Hall offers a historical perspective. "A long time ago, someone gave our ghost that name. He could possibly have been one of the victims of the tornado that went through here in 1936, and he was brought here and never left. Almost three hundred people were killed or maimed. They used the Lyric as an operating room. They took the doors off the county courthouse across the street and used them as litters to bring the wounded and injured over here to operate on them." Hall passes on a few more grisly tales. "There are rumors that the limbs of the victims that were cut off during the operations . . . were thrown . . . under the stage." Hall's face compresses into a grimace. "I don't know if there is any truth to that. It does kind of smell kind of off down there."

On April 5, 1936, the fourth deadliest tornado in United States history slammed into Tupelo. The massive funnel skipped over the downtown business district, but to the town's horror, it zeroed in on the residential areas. There was little to no warning. The tornado leveled homes and wiped out entire families. The death toll hovered around 230, but this only accounted for white families. The actual number may be significantly higher as death tolls among African Americans were not reported or recorded until the late forties. Singling out Antoine from among the hundreds of dead, dying, or injured in the theatre that dreadful evening would be a formidable task.

Booth says that over the years there have been several potential characters cast in the role of the theatre's grouchy ghost. "Some people think he may be someone that died during the tornado, others believe it might be a previous caretaker of the building who has never left, never went away. No one really knows. I've been around for eighteen years, and he's always been called Antoine. I can't say anymore, except things happen. When the Tupelo Community Theatre bought the building twenty-six years ago, I guess we inherited the ghost."

Lagniappe: The sturdy Art Deco building at 200 North Broadway has always been in the spotlight. Built in 1912 by R. F. Goodlett, the Cosmos (the original name) was designed for live vaudeville acts. In the 1930s, as vaudeville took a back seat to "talkies," the M. A. Lightman Company reconfigured it as a movie theatre. Its popularity grew along with local lore that the town's most famous native son, Elvis Presley, stole his first kiss in the balcony of the Lyric movie theatre. Sadly, by 1984 the theatre fell into decline. It was abandoned, and its finale was to be a date with the wrecking ball. A reprieve arrived in the form of grants, gifts, pledges, and community and state support. The Lyric was restored and is now home to one of the finest amateur theatrical venues in the South.

11

Rosedale

No sound rings forth from the campanile at Rosedale; it is a bell tower without bells. The design is pure Italian and most closely resembles Giotto's Bell Tower, the freestanding campanile of Florence Cathedral on the Piazza del Dumo in Italy. In 1856, when Dr. William Topp built his showplace in Columbus, Mississippi, he knew what he wanted and got it. The good doctor's prescription? The illusion of a bell tower as the central focus of his mansion, minus the deafening noise a cacophony of bells would create. What Dr. Topp could not foresee was that his bell tower would provide the perfect nest for a fledgling spirit.

With glowing skin, Leigh Imes wears her glossy brown hair in a shoulder-length flip, and even with her plaid shirttail hanging out over skinny jeans, she has that casual-put-together finesse of a runway model. Together with her husband, Gene, Leigh is the owner and proud restorer of Rosedale. "We bought the house twelve years ago. We had a hard time deciding what to do. Dixie and Carl Butler restored Temple Heights, another historic home in Columbus, and Carl came over here and told us that we really needed to redo the house in the period that it was first built. So we did. For those first seven years, we collected the furniture, and then we moved out for four years so the renovations could be completed. We hired George Fore, an architectural conservator from North Carolina, and Skip Tuminello, from Vicksburg, as the architect for the addition in back." And the hauntings began.

Leigh stands in the spacious upstairs hallway. It is larger than most bedrooms. The main stairwell is at the back end of the hall. At the opposite end is a door to a second landing with a separate staircase for the

Rosedale mansion sits in isolated splendor on a rural road in Columbus.

two-storied bell tower. Leigh pieces together the peculiar unraveling of one haunted evening. "We'd been to J. Broussard's restaurant to eat that night. While the renovations were going on, Skip Tuminello slept in the guest bedroom, closest to the tower door. Skip was asleep when we got back. He came down the next morning and said he heard a lady and a child in the hall outside his room, and they woke him up. He said it was two distinct voices, an older woman and a little girl. They were playing a game. He didn't know what game, but the little girl was giggling and the old woman was talking to her. He opened his door to look. There was nobody there. The voices stopped and he went back to bed. This went on three different times in the middle of the night." Leigh hesitates before going on. "It was so real to Skip that he even accused us of tricking him. He kept asking, 'Are you playing a joke on me? Are you sure you all weren't up there?' And we said, 'Why would we be playing in the hall?' And he just said that he thought we all had to be up to something."

Leigh reviewed any other sources that might be mistaken for voices. "Our daughter Megan was asleep, and there was no older woman staying in the house. We keep the door to the tower open from time to time. I've heard the wind blow and shake and all that, and I've heard creaks, but Skip insisted it was two voices and they were playing. He didn't seem to be terrified by it; it just bothered him enough that he told us, 'I can't stay here anymore.' He would stay with a friend in Columbus while he was working here, and he never spent another night at Rosedale."

Skip's experience validates that of a longtime resident of Columbus. "I have a friend," remembers Leigh, "whose husband as a teenager would ride by Rosedale quite a bit. He would say that as he passed he would always check out the window on the top level of the tower, and when he did, he could see a little girl walking up and down the staircase." Leigh catches herself midthought. "That is strange because Skip Tuminello heard a little girl outside his bedroom door, which is right by the landing to the tower. It's weird; two different people talking about the same little girl ghost, decades apart, and Skip, not even knowing anything about the earlier stories."

Rosedale's tower affords a 360-degree view of the surrounding fields. The house sits a good football field back from the nearest road. There are few trees to obstruct the street-level view of the front of Rosedale. French doors on the lower tower level open on to a Juliet balcony with a wrought-iron railing. The upper tier of the tower has four pairs of arched windows facing the four compass points. The stairs inside the campanile pass directly in front of the glass of the upper and lower tiers.

"The children who lived at the Palmer House would also talk about the little girl ghost in the tower," admits Leigh. The residential dorms of Palmer House are like box seats overlooking the pond off the right wing of Rosedale. Palmer House was founded in 1895 as a place for "children with no where else to turn." By 1902, the eighteen-acre facility housed forty "social orphans." Tales of Rosedale's ghost are a common topic among Palmer House alumni, now numbering one thousand strong. "The kids staying there would say that they could see a light on in the tower windows when the house was vacant, and the little girl would go up and down the stairs."

Leigh decided to give the sight lines a little test run. "I actually went outside at night to see if you could spot a figure in the landing." Leigh concedes that anyone mortal or otherwise, ascending or descending these stairs, would be visible from the street. She is just sad that her timing is off. "My husband has said he wished he could see her, but neither of us have. I guess we are not susceptible; still there must be something to it with so many people telling the same story."

Leigh and Gene Imes are the sixth family to own Rosedale. "The first owners, the Topps, had five children here. In 1904, they sold the house to W. V. Grace. The Graces lived here for a very long time, forty years. This house has always been a home for children." On the back stairwell that connects the original house to the new addition, a wall of photos chronicles happy moments in the life of daughter Megan Imes. Her infectious smile shines through from baby pictures to a more adventurous young girl on horseback jumping fences. A proud mother, Leigh extends her arms as if to embrace all the little ones who ever ran through the mansion. "Children were all over this place all the time; if you talk to anybody that's from Columbus, they'll say, 'Oh, yeah, I used to play at that house.'" Leigh continues the happy tradition. "Life is too short not to enjoy it. My daughter had a slumber party. All the girls put on socks and slid up and down the front hall like it was an ice-skating rink. Children haven't changed at all. If something gets broken, it's bad, but things happen; you move on." Leigh's voice has an inviting, intimate, Jackie Kennedy-whisperlike quality. She is thoughtful. "So I guess it was natural that Skip Tuminello heard children's voices in the house. I wish I could hear the little girl's voice."

A tiny ball of gray-and-white shaggy fur scampers into the front hall. Leigh bends over to pet Harvey, a Havanese puppy. Harvey is a perfect fit for this Italian mansion. Harvey shadows Leigh, but sometimes he struggles to keep up; his stubby paws support an eight-pound body barely nine inches off the floor. This time Harvey is knocked off course by a stealthy calico cat hell bent on crossing the black-and-white, diamond-patterned floor. "We have a Noah's ark here," says Leigh, scooping up Harvey in her arms. "I've heard that animals are more aware of spirits." Harvey gives Leigh a look of pure puppy devotion. "My cats will freeze as they are climbing up the stairs. I don't see anything, and I can't figure out what they are staring at."

Leigh Imes is not troubled by any potential ghosts that came to the home before her; however, she does own up to a mild form of *furniphobia*. In February of 2009, *Fear of Furniture,* an animated documentary, captured the anguish of a man on a new-furniture-buying expedition; he saw the looming purchases as a symbol of submission to a life of drudgery. Leigh has a leery, getting-to-know-you, cooling-off period with recent antique acquisitions at Rosedale, where an unsurpassed collection of American-made antiques grace the halls.

If ghoulies and ghosties can take over rooms and towers, why can't they hitch a ride inside an armoire, burrow in a draw, or wrap their tenacious spirits around the sinewy curve of a cabriole leg? "You know how sometimes someone can buy an old piece of furniture and bring something with them to your house?" Leigh's question is rhetorical. "That always kind of freaked me out at first when we bought this furniture. . . . I always worried where the pieces came from and what might be attached to them." Leigh's mother has similar concerns.

Against a backdrop of gold *fleur-de-lis* on deep-red wallpaper, the Gothic Revival bed in the guest room is breathtaking. The spires on the canopy soar to the fourteen-foot ceiling, and the headboard and footboard are designed with carved vaulted arches reminiscent of cathedral architecture. "My mother will not sleep in this bed. She thinks it's a beautiful bed, but she gets a funny feeling from it." Leigh makes a face. "She says the bed is creepy; it bothers her." Leigh is unsure whether it is a combination of bed and bedroom that causes her mother to sleep elsewhere. "This was the room that Skip Tuminello slept in when he heard the little girl and the old woman playing outside his door, but this is a different bed. The bed Skip slept in is now in my daughter Megan's room. One of the previous owners, Mr. Grace, died in that bedroom."

And while Leigh swears that "nothing strange has every happened in my daughter's bedroom," the complicated origins of Rosedale's two talking ghosts persist when the present owner says, "We think the older woman is Mrs. Grace because we've heard that her ghost haunts here, but I've yet to know who the little girl is."

During the restoration process, Gene and Leigh Imes found numerous old photos to guide them. They would have preferred to salvage all of the ancillary buildings that had been on the grounds, but most were torn down prior to their arrival. Their new pool house sits on the same footprint of the original kitchen. "We found a little bit of the brick walkway and pieces of china scattered about."

The guest bedroom with its Gothic bed.

Although the historic images of Rosedale also offered clues to the location of the servant quarters, Leigh's visceral experience was more personal. "I walked outside in the back . . . this is kind of weird . . . it smelled like somebody struck a match: the smell of sulfur, real strong. I had this image of the servants, and it made me wonder about how they were treated because their living quarters were back there."

Although Leigh claims she is not as tuned in to the supernatural as other visitors to the house, she can easily run through a checklist of the inexplicable. "I have been in other parts of the house and heard the front door slam shut when it is already closed. One time the alarm was even beeping and no one was there. I got really upset; it was out of place. You see shadows from time to time as you enter a room. It's hard to tell if your eyes are playing tricks on you or not. And this house feels real warm to me sometimes in certain rooms. It's not anything I am afraid of; just maybe it could be someone who's lived here before."

Leigh Imes is clear on one thing. "This is a historic home to me, not a haunted house. If there is something here, it likes us I guess."

Lagniappe: Rosedale is open to the public only by appointment or during the Columbus Spring Pilgrimage tour of homes. Leigh, Gene, and Megan live at Rosedale full time. The campanile, the bell tower, is an amazing space to watch the sunset, drink a glass of wine, and enjoy the bucolic view all the way out to the Tombigbee River. It is also the perfect spot for a little girl ghost to hide and keep an eye on visitors below.

Temple Heights on a bluff in Columbus.

12

Temple Heights

What's happening to us?
—from the movie *The Amityville Horror*

In the 1979 paranormal blockbuster movie *The Amityville Horror,* actor James Brolin is losing his mind. He and his wife have just purchased an old deserted home, and it's possessed. A door blows off its hinges, windows slam shut, ooze drips from nail heads in the walls, swarms of flies invade a room, and malevolent manifestations stalk the house. The movie is based on the actual experiences of newlyweds George and Kathy Lutz.

"When we first went to see *The Amityville Horror,* everybody in the audience was scared. Carl and I just laughed." Dixie and her late husband, Carl Butler, found the movie's paranormal antics paled in comparison to the haunted happenings at Temple Heights, their historic home in Columbus. "I mean, I even have stuff that oozes out of the walls. I just had it repaired again this year. You scrape it out, put some mud on it, smooth it out, and then its back." This former elementary school principal presents the facts in a manner that leaves no room for doubt.

In some aspects, Dixie and Carl Butler's lives mirrored those of George and Kathy Lutz, the couple who purchased the Amityville house. George and Kathy were newlyweds when they first saw High Hopes, the house at 112 Ocean Drive on the south shore of Long Island, New York. Although the Dutch colonial sat vacant and was in need of repair, the Lutzes fell in love with the house's gambrel (barn-shaped) roof and a pair of quarter-circle windows on the end. On the market for a bargain price of $80,000, the Lutz family jumped at the opportunity to snag their dream house for $40,000 below the appraised value.

Dixie Butler's initial reaction to Temple Heights in Columbus was not so favorable, but like High Hopes in Amityville, the price was right, and Dixie's future husband made an offer she couldn't refuse. "Carl had already seen the house. We were both grad students in Nashville. One day he drew the floor plans for me and asked, 'Do you think you'd like to live in it?' And I said, 'Do you mean with you?' And he said yes, and I said yes." After the unusual marriage proposal, Carl warned Dixie, "Now, don't get your hopes up. It is really going to be in bad shape." Dixie is forthright. "I have to tell you, it was so much worse than I possibly could have imagined. It really was. It was really pretty dreary when I first saw it on a cold November day."

In an interview for *Reflections: Homes and History of Columbus, Mississippi,* by Sylvia Higginbotham, Carl Butler describes the circumstances leading to the purchase. "I'd always been interested in historic properties and knew about Temple Heights but was told it was uninhabitable. It was in terrible shape visually; it had not been painted in forty years. . . . After Dixie and I got engaged, we decided we wanted this house and made the commitment to restore it." Owner Kirk Egger cut the young couple an unbelievable deal. "Since we were both in graduate school in Nashville—Dixie at Peabody, I was at Vanderbilt—he let us pay one thousand dollars down."

Dixie's hair has turned a soft gray now, but she remembers the excitement of that first home purchase. "We bought Temple Heights the last day of 1967. We didn't have to pay any more until we were out of school. We got married in 1968 and started living here in 1969."

Both couples, the Butlers and the Lutzes, would soon come to question their decisions. When George and Kathy Lutz purchased High Hopes, the real estate agent disclosed that on November 13, 1974, a father, mother, and their four children—two girls and two boys—were murdered in the house. Many potential buyers were scared off. However, George Lutz was not dissuaded, saying, "Houses don't have memories." But at the urging of a family friend, he invited a priest to bless the house. In subsequent television interviews with talk show host Merv Griffin and ABC's Elizabeth Vargas, George says the blessing had the opposite effect.

Father Delany believed the house had an evil spirit and tried to perform an exorcism. Kathy had nightmares about the murders. Their daughter was convinced she had a ghost, a malevolent spirit, for a playmate. George's work suffered, and the evil vibes in the house repulsed his business partner's wife.

Dixie scoffs at the movie version's exaggerated portrayal of what may have happened to the Lutzes. "I've had people who had *real* experiences. When we first got married, we would bring Mrs. Wakefield, our landlady from Nashville, with us. She stayed in this room [second-floor guest bedroom], and she saw a little wispy thing coming down the steps from the third floor to the second-floor landing. So she closed this door [and] put a chair against it. She said later that that probably wouldn't do any good. And she was a really intelligent lady not prone to over imagination." A shadow of a smile tugs at the corners of Dixie's lips. "And we knew it wasn't either Carl or I that she saw because we aren't *wispy.*" When asked to describe the ghostly form, Dixie says that Mrs. Wakefield "couldn't put her finger on whether it was a child or an adult. I have had some people stay in here, they felt a presence, but they couldn't identify it either."

Dixie, on the other hand, is confident she knows who it is. "I think it is Elizabeth. One of the ladies that lived here was named Elizabeth Kennebrew. She lived and died here. When things happen here, we just say that is Miss Elizabeth."

The wispy ghostlike figure was identified by someone who knew Elizabeth well. "We were having a dinner party here," says Dixie. "One of my friends went upstairs to use the bathroom [until recently the only bathroom in the house was on the second floor]. My friend heard somebody outside waiting. After she rejoined us at the table, she said, 'I just had the strangest thing happen. When I was leaving the bathroom, I passed somebody in the hall, and I thought she was waiting for me to get out.'" Dixie says there were no other guests in the house except the ones seated at the table, so they asked the woman who had just come from the bathroom to tell them more about the person she saw. Everyone in the dining room was astonished as an older friend of Dixie's exclaimed, "You're describing Elizabeth Kennebrew. I knew Elizabeth."

At High Hopes in Amityville, the manifestations, as depicted in the horror movie, had no intention of waiting their turn. The Lutzes called in a second priest to cleanse the house. This exorcism also failed. After twenty-eight days, the Lutz family fled Amityville and moved to another state, their dreams and hopes in ruins. At Temple Heights, Carl and Dixie Butler were not so easily dissuaded.

The Butlers handled their ghosts and tackled the restoration with equal aplomb. "Since we knew we couldn't afford to redo everything, we could mop the floor and we could put Johnson's paste wax on it. We found that we could paint a room in a weekend, so we would come down from Nashville and paint over whatever was here, knowing that we would come back and sheetrock when we could afford it, but at least it made the rooms feel livable," explains Dixie.

As for the ghosts and other questionable activities around the house, they addressed them each in turn. "My goodness, we heard noises when there was no one around. Doors opened and closed by themselves. One time there was a big crash when Don Schollander, the Olympic swimming star, and his wife were staying with us." As the local high-school swim coach with an impressive winning record, Carl Butler had persuaded the four-time gold-medal winner of the 1964 Summer Olympics to give a clinic for the swim team. "Don and his wife were by the pool at the house; we were getting ready to have lunch, and we heard the crash. We never could find anything that fell to make such a loud noise."

Random sounds are a common occurrence at Temple Heights. "We will hear music or voices, and you'll think you've left the radio or the television on upstairs, and there won't be anybody. We climb the stairs to the second floor and the lights turn on and off."

There is one piece of the paranormal puzzle that annoys Dixie more than the others. "Carl's parents were staying here. I had gone to bed, and they were downstairs. Out of curiosity, Mr. Butler asked Carl if we knew which rooms the Kennebrew sisters used." Dixie walks over to the *faux bois,* paneled door in the guest bedroom. "We knew this was Laura Kennebrew's room because she wrote her name on it; her signature was etched into the door." Dixie's tone is precise. "Carl brought his parents up to this room to show them where Laura had signed her name, and he couldn't find it. The master bedroom is the room next to this. I was reading, and Carl called, 'Dixie, come show Mother and Daddy where Laura wrote her name. I can't find it.'" Frustration filters in. "I couldn't find it either. After they left, I got a flashlight and I went to every door in the house looking for Laura's name." Dixie briefly tried to convince herself that maybe she and Carl had gotten confused about which door had the name; it had been awhile since they had looked at it. Then years of listening to students try to wiggle out of a situation when they are caught in the act kicked in. "It was right across here." Dixie indicates a spot at eye level on the inside of Laura's bedroom door. "It was in big print. We had shown it to a lot of people before Carl's parents asked about it." Dixie refuses to entertain the possibility that she might have been hallucinating. "No, it was there. And it has never reappeared. There are a lot of things you just can't explain. You just have to accept."

Elizabeth Kennebrew had a different view. She refused to accept the apology from a suitor who stood her up. Dixie carefully unfolds a handwritten letter. The pages are delicate parchment paper. They crinkle as she smoothes them out.

Laura Kennebrew's bedroom where her name disappeared from the door.

Dear Lizette,

I know that you will never speak to me again and I think you have a right not to after what happened last evening. I feel as if I never can look at you in the face again. You may not believe me, but I never had anything to happen that bothered me more, but listen, I will explain. Yesterday, a week ago, I made a date with Miss Haley to accompany her to church, but had forgotten all about it when I asked you if I may walk home with you . . . I want to ask you to forgive me and promise you it will never happen again. Will you?. . . Please let me know for I am bothered to death. Hoping you will have compassion on me.

I am so ever your sincere friend, Joseph Wilbur, September, 1908

Elizabeth spurned her would-be suitor. "She remained an old maid," says Dixie. Elizabeth never married, but her mother's will provided for Elizabeth and her sisters, Laura, Daisy, Ruth, and Jessie. "Mrs.

Dixie Butler reads Joseph's letter to Lizette.

Kennebrew's will said that as long as there was an unmarried daughter, the house couldn't be sold." Elizabeth was able to live out the remainder of her days at Temple Heights.

Now that Elizabeth inhabits another realm, free of the physical restraints of old age, she seems to enjoy floating down from the upper floors to the lower. Dixie Butler is pleased to have her.

Downstairs in the brilliant blue foyer another woman's signature has caused some confusion. "Mrs. Francis Jane Fontaine owned this house from 1867 to 1887. Her daughter, Annie, scratched her name in the pane of glass to the right of the front door. People say she scratched it with her diamond ring." Dixie Butler stares at the flourishes in the lower panel of the glass sidelights on the right side of the door. "You can't really do that unless you take the diamond out of the ring. I don't know how she did that; if I knew I would put my name in here." A broad smile brightens her face. Dixie is ever vigilant about Annie's signature. "This glass has cracked, and I hope it lasts under my watch. I am the only one who washes it." Unlike Elizabeth's signature on the bedroom door, Dixie intends to make sure Annie's signature stays put. "I have a sense of all of the people who have lived here. I am in awe of their stories."

Temple Heights is on the National Register of Historic Places and a featured stop on the annual Columbus Spring Pilgrimage Home, Garden and Church Tour. In 1847, Richard T. Brownrigg, a native of Edenton, North Carolina, arrived in Columbus and soon made his fortune as a cotton planter. Brownrigg built Temple Heights as a singular testament to his achievements.

"We had a party at our house in 1987 to celebrate its 150th birthday." Dixie Butler is beaming. "People came from all over the country. Since that time, we came to know a descendant of one of the former occupants on the property, Dr. Morris Henderson of Richmond. He teaches at Virginia Commonwealth University." Dixie is excited to have a fellow scholar come to visit and share his family's story of Temple Heights.

"During Columbus's annual pilgrimage, I had someone in the kitchen playing the part of General Brownrigg. Dr. Henderson sat down next to him, and they kind of fed off of each other, telling the history of the families who lived here. People were fascinated." For Dixie Butler, knowing that Temple Heights serves a place where the past is rekindled in the present day makes all her efforts worthwhile.

Lagniappe: The history of Temple Heights is well documented, and despite all that has happened in the ensuing years, Dixie Butler is not afraid. "It's not a spooky house. It is a friendly house so whatever is here, I am comfortable with."

In 2015, after forty-six years of hosting visitors and ghosts, Dixie Butler announced she was leaving. Calling the move "bittersweet," Butler added, "I am delighted with the people who are going to get the house." Miss Elizabeth Kennebrew, the resident ghost of Temple Heights, is grateful as well that the new owners will be equally accommodating.

13

Waverley

Yet, with a stern delight and strange
I saw the spirit-stirring change.
As warr'd the wind with wave and wood
Upon the ruined tower I stood.
—Sir Walter Scott, *Waverley*

A traveling salesman spins a whopper of a tale to Robert and Madonna Snow about a haunted house in the deep weeds of Clay County near West Point, Mississippi; lost on a dirt road, he spied a decrepit mansion in the tangled overgrowth. The Snows, antique dealers from Philadelphia, Mississippi, are intrigued. They hop a ferry across the Tombigbee River and clamber up a knoll. Poking through the treetop is an octagonal cupola crowning an H-shaped, four-storied, eight-thousand-square-foot behemoth. Thirty-eight-year-old Robert and thirty-six-year-old "Donna" are in love.

Three months later, in October of 1962, Robert and Donna sell their antiques shop, farm, and timberland to raise money to purchase Waverley, an 1852 antebellum mansion. They pack up their children—Allen, eleven; Melanie, seven; and little Cindy, five—and move in. An adult Melanie Snow remembers it as more like camping out. "We loaded up our old station wagon and threw caution to the winds. My parents weren't money people; they had all they could do to buy the house; they had no idea how they would be able to restore it." The family pulled up and hacked their way to the rotting porch. The front steps were missing, and the front door had been wedged ajar. Honeysuckle vines snaked up over the house,

107

Waverley Plantation amid acres of forest land in West Point.

and branches poked through broken windows. A few faded-green shutters dangled askew while the rest lay scattered on the ground.

Conditions inside were even more deplorable. A moldy mat of leaves, branches, and human refuse carpeted the floor. An infestation of possums, squirrels, birds, bats, insects, and one very loud ghost had settled in. "We slept on mattresses in the dining room because we couldn't even get into the bedrooms on the second floor." The family's sleep was interrupted by sonic boomlike crashes from above that felt like the ceiling was caving in.

The heavy-handed, foot-stomping ghost was the least of their problems. "We had no electricity or plumbing; we hauled water up and down the muddy dirt roads, miles back and forth from the nearest neighbors." But there was plenty of reading material.

Graffiti covered every square inch of the walls. There were thousands of names. During the fifty years that Waverley sat vacant, campers, hunters, and fishermen used it as a way stop. Curiosity seekers filtered in and out and scrawled their names on every available space. "Mississippi State University in Starkville, thirty miles away, sent their pledges over here for decades. If you could spend the night in the spook house, you could be in the club." Melanie laughs, "That's the truth. The worst thing we found scribbled on the walls was *'For a good time, call Lulu in Cowtown, Texas.'* She must have been a bad, bad, girl." Rather than tear out the old plaster to remove all of the signatures and writing on the walls, the Snows worked for more than two years cleaning out each name. "Every crevice, every crack, we worked with boxes of toothbrushes, toothpicks, and wooden kitchen matches to remove the wood daubers. Irishmen worked over two years to install the plaster and it took us two and a half years to clean and repair it."

Although pounded by the elements, the house was structurally sound and survived the onslaught of five decades of uninvited visitors. Other than the wall-to-wall graffiti, there was little vandalism. In the rotunda, a matching pair of self-supporting staircases curves upwards to cantilevered balconies on the second, third, and fourth floors. Of the 718 hand-turned, mahogany spindles, only one was missing. Less than twenty windowpanes were broken, and there was only one BB hole in the house. "No one took the marble mantels; there were eight in the house," reports a blue-eyed, red-headed Melanie. "They left the original French gasoliers in each of the rooms and the large, gold-leaf mirrors."

Miraculously, Waverley also escaped going up in flames. "We have a number of photographs of this entrance hall, and in the rotunda, someone had placed a big metal barrel. They had campfires inside to keep warm. They had drinking parties." Melanie testifies to the horrific dangers. "We found thousands of cigarette butts in the house. The rotunda is open; it goes sixty-five feet straight up. It was designed to carry the heat up and then be let out of the sixteen windows in the cupola. If a fire had gotten out of control here, Waverley would be nothing more than ashes."

The Snow family believes that the ghosts guarded the house. "We have had so many people tells us through the years that they would sneak into Waverley to go ghost hunting or picnicking, and any time somebody was up to no good, or thinking about maybe stealing a wall sconce, there would be loud noises like shotguns and boards popping together, it would scare them and they would run away."

There is one little spirit that seems to be particularly active, and

Melanie knows her well. As a child, Melanie roamed in and out of every inch, every hidden corner, and every obscure cubbyhole of Waverly. She is a gifted storyteller. "Legend has it that the little ghost girl has been here over one hundred years, long before we ever heard of Waverley. No one knows for sure who she is, but we make the bed in the ghost room, the first room at the top of the stairs, and when we go in there, the imprint of her little body is on the bed; the bedspread is wrinkled, just like a little child has crawled up to nap or play. Many people hear her. We've been at Waverley for forty-eight years. I've heard her. My mother heard her; the family has heard her a number of times. She's in the gardens and in the woods and in the house in that ghost room. A sweet angelic voice calls, *'Mama, Mama.'* We believe she is the guardian angel that protected the house all the years it was vacant and protects the house today."

Having inspired many love stories, Waverley is an unusual haunted house. "This was the *play* house for the area and everybody courted out here and wrote on the walls and woodwork who knew who. This past weekend, a lady on a tour said that when she and her husband were courting out here, they wrote their names in that room [the main parlor]. My mom always said we knew every love affair for fifty years. When people in the community come back to visit now, they tell us that they were proposed to out here, their children were conceived out here." Melanie jumps to their defense. "They never dreamed of doing anything wrong to the house. They will say, 'I crossed the ferry on the river just to look around and met this darling boy over there looking around, and we had a picnic, and we fell in love, and we've been married for forty-nine years.' It's a love house. A house of romance that's for sure."

Col. George Hampton Young and his wife, Lucy Woodson Watkins Young, designed the house with a romantic theme from its inception. Brackets of lyres frame the front door. Seven of the ten Young children said their vows under the framed archway of the "wedding alcove" in the parlor. "The little babies were also baptized here. This was like a little chapel. The Youngs built it knowing they would hold all of the family's important moments here." The tradition lives on. "Since we've been here, we've had a number of wedding proposals; sometimes they'll drop to their knees in the wedding alcove or under the magnolia tree or in the original lover's lane to the left of the house." The trail Melanie indicates winds past

The bedroom where the little girl ghost likes to nap.

Lyres frame the front entrance of Waverley.

the house into a secluded glen. The lovers are probably blissfully unaware that they are stepping over the grave of Maj. John Pytchlyn. His ghostly gallivants take him on spectral jaunts through Waverley's grounds.

John "Jack" Pytchlyn was an Englishman by birth who lived among the Mississippi Choctaws and served as an interpreter for the United States government after the Revolutionary War. He married a Choctaw woman. He loved riding his horse along the Tombigbee River, near the future landing of Colonel Young's plantation. Pytchlyn died in 1835, and his gravesite was the vacant field where Waverley would one day stand. The funeral was conducted in the Choctaw warrior tradition. His rifle, boots, and saddle were deposited with his coffin. Mrs. Pytchlyn called for his horse to be killed and buried in the grave with his master. Judge Samuel Gholson intervened on behalf of the horse and assured the widow that a horse befitting the major's rank would surely be furnished by "the Great Spirit in the Happy Hunting Grounds." The widow Pytchlyn acquiesced and ordered a brick wall to be erected to protect the grave. She made semiannual visits to check on the gravesite. After reports of the grave being disturbed, the neighbors noticed that the widow's visits had ceased. Local gossip speculated that Mrs. Pytchlyn had removed the body to Indian Territory. No evidence of the brick wall or the grave remains, but at night, the faint sound of pounding hoofs rises to a crescendo, the earth is said to shudder, and a powerful whoosh of wind carries a phantom horse and rider past Waverley.

The Waverley mansion sits back from a narrow country road. The cupola is the only visible sign that something magnificent lies beyond the surrounding forty-acre forest. During the era of the Young family, the cotton plantation operated as a self-sustaining village with 50,000 acres of cleared land. Melanie lists a few of the operations. "There were grist mills, saw mills, molasses mills, a brick kiln, a cotton gin, an ice house, and a huge leather tannery operation. They manufactured for sale straw hats, leather hats, and boots for men, women, and children."

Colonel Young kept a desk in the cupola where he could see for miles. Melanie has read many of the first owner's journals. "He named his plantation Waverley after the title of his favorite novel by author and poet Sir Walter Scott."

The Youngs lived on a palatial level, yet there were also moments of tragedy. In 1836, George and Lucy and the first born of their ten children moved into a two-story log cabin where they could watch the construction of their grand mansion rise from dream to reality. Poor Lucy had little time to savor its magnificence. She died in 1852, the year the mansion was completed.

Exploring Waverley is a treasure hunt on an immense scale. A chip of red brick in the front yard might be from the brick wall that once enclosed the grave of Major Pytchlyn, the phantom rider. Across the country road, broken slabs of marble hint at the luxurious lifestyle of the Youngs and the visit of one famous spy. "At one of the artesian wells on the property, Colonel Young built an Italian marble-lined swimming pool with bathhouses for men and women. People have taken most of the marble over the years, but few of them know about one lady who came here to hide out."

Melanie's voice drops to a whisper as if the woman's secret identity must still be protected. "Belle Edmundson was a female Civil War spy. She's been called the lost heroine of the Confederacy. She smuggled money and mail under her petticoats. There was a letter issued for her arrest in Memphis so she came to Waverley as a refugee. She was friends with Lucy [the Young's daughter named after her mother] and stayed for six months. Belle kept her diary here, and she wrote, *'On hot humid afternoons, the ladies went down early to bathe but did not linger long because the gentlemen were anxious.'*"

Colonel Young loved to experiment. A copper-domed brick retort near the house burned rich pinewood to produce pine-rosin gas, which fueled the gasoliers. "Colonel Young had lighting before anyone else." Melanie has read the accounts. "People at that time wrote in their journals about riding out to Waverley by horseback to see the lights, see the gasoliers. It was a novelty." The gasolier in the master bedroom went from novelty to nest when baby squirrels were discovered in the glass globes by the Snow children after they moved in. "We called this room the Possum Condominium because possums liked the chandeliers as much as the squirrels. We'd take a little stick and the possums would wrap their tails around it, and we'd carry possums all over the house." Melanie nods her head in satisfaction. "The ghost girl did a good job protecting everything, because even with all the animals running around here, none of the glass globes were broken."

Waverley Plantation was the social center of the region with weekly dances and masquerade balls in the rotunda. The pink flounce of a taffeta ball gown, golden curls caught up in ribbon and lace, a gentleman's starched white collar, and a red ruby necklace—fleeting images of the family and their many guests have been seen in the mirrors. "This mirror was cracked at a dance held here during the Civil War but not from vandalism." Melanie is in the rotunda. A jagged crack runs the length of a gilded, pier mirror mounted on the wall. "It is documented in one of the old journals that during a big dance here, candles were placed in front of the mirror to add a warm glow to the party." One candle was too close to the leaded glass. "When it overheated, it popped so loud that in the journal notation it said, *'We thought we were under attack; we secured the house and the women.'*" Melanie laughs. "I bet the petticoats were flying."

The four-story main rotunda with the cracked pier mirror and ghostly images.

After a thorough search of the grounds, the men found nothing; they realized the sound came from the crack in the mirror, and the ball resumed. The cracked glass is said to give a distorted image of phantom dancers.

Melanie steps into the parlor and stares into the mirror over the white-marble fireplace mantel. "This mirror holds fifty years of faces; thousands of faces are reflected back if you look hard enough." Young brides with tentative smiles; stern-faced grooms; a baby, mouth open in rage at the cold christening water on its forehead; and a distraught father and husband mourning his beloved Lucy lying in a coffin in the alcove. They are all here: the hunters and fishermen, the college pledges, the lovers, and the vagrants.

Even the spindles on the cantilevered second-floor balconies harbor a tale, one linked to the identity of the little girl ghost. During the Civil War when Memphis and New Orleans were under attack, Waverley housed dozens of refugee girls from those cities. They doubled up in the bedrooms, slept in the guesthouses, and on cots in the parlor. The Young boys—Watt, Valley, Beverly, Thomas, Erskine, James, and William—had joined the Confederacy. Colonel Young stayed behind to protect his plantation and supply the Confederate troops with food, horses, and clothing.

At the neighboring Burt plantation, all the men had gone to war. Dr. Burt's daughter and two granddaughters were left behind. Colonel Young sent his house servants to bring them to Waverley for the duration. Nine-year-old Carrie Hampton contracted diphtheria. Five days later, eighteen-month-old Cynthia Hampton joined her sister in death. Melanie Snow and historian/tour guide James Denning do not know with 100 percent certainty how Cynthia died. However, Melanie and James are inclined to believe that baby Cynthia was the curious toddler who slipped away one day, stuck her head through the spindles of the second-floor railing, and broke her neck. All that can be confirmed is that the event happened and that both of Susan Burt Hampton's little girls died at Waverley. "That's factual," confirms Melanie. "It's in the family records."

Those who have seen Waverley's little girl ghost describe her as being quite small. "We have the birth and death records of the Young children and grandchildren. They all lived to be adults, so we know the spirit haunting the house is not one of them." The Snow family can only

The mirror in the front parlor that reflects hundreds of ghostly faces.

surmise that the one who protects the house and is still calling for her mama is likely little Cynthia Hampton.

After the war, all but one of the Young boys returned home safely. The girls married and moved away as did three of the remaining six boys. Colonel Young died in 1888. James and Billy lived on at Waverley. James spent his bachelor days reading the Bible. William, or "Billy," the youngest, sought livelier pursuits.

Captain Billy served for a time as Waverley's postmaster. When the post office near the river landing closed, Billy took the walnut secretary and installed it in Waverley's library. A note from Billy dated December 26, 1898, reads *"No mail today. Messenger got drunk."* This is an ironic commentary from a man with a reputation for overindulgence. The library also features a silver dipper passed from friend to friend during Billy's infamous late-night poker parties. Luke Richardson, the last houseboy employed at Waverley, returned during the restoration by Robert and Donna Snow. Richardson's account validates history. As a twelve-year-old, he and the staff "stayed up all night serving food and drink to the poker-playing guests."

When Billy died in 1913, distant nieces, nephews, and cousins inherited the estate. "As with the best of families," explains Melanie, "they argued for fifty years about what to do with the house. Waverley sat vacant for half a century."

In his eighteenth-century novel titled *Waverley,* English author Sir Walter Scott could have been describing twentieth-century conditions at Waverley in Mississippi when he wrote, *"The very trees mourned for her, for their leaves dropped around her without a gust of wind; and indeed she looked like one that would never see them green again."*

The Snows see their role at Waverley as caretakers of this National Historic Landmark and National Restoration Award winner. They are grateful to all of the ghosts who ensured that there would be a Waverley for years to come, but they retain a special fondness for their little guardian angel and encourage her to stick around.

Donna Snow's entire face pivots inside this portrait.

Lagniappe: The Snow family has created a mysterious aura of their own. When Madonna "Donna" Gutherie Snow first stepped into Waverley in 1962, she described it as "a magnificent mess" and then began a lifelong restoration. Like Lucy Young before her, matriarch Donna Snow had only a short time to enjoy Waverley in full bloom. With a face full of emotion, Donna's daughter, Melanie, remembers, "We finished the last room, the parlor, eighteen years ago, just before Mom died; she was able to see all the bricks restored and all the house done."

When Donna Snow died, the Mississippi legislature observed a moment of prayer and passed a resolution citing her work promoting Mississippi through Waverley. The Snow family commissioned a painting to honor Donna. The portrait hangs above the mantel in the dining room. Passing in front of the portrait, Donna follows you. Her head turns. "We watch people walking by; they stop and have the most perplexed look on their faces. As you start at one end of the dining room, mother is facing right. As you continue, she faces left." Madonna Snow, dressed in a black, lace, high-collared ball gown is seated. Her hands gently clasp a dozen long-stemmed yellow roses. Her oval face is in quiet repose. If you stand directly in front of the portrait, her brown eyes look past you to a view of the gardens through the windows. But if you move, so does she. There are no hidden wires or digital special effects. The illusion is magical.

Since 1852, Waverley had been home to only two families, the Youngs and the Snows. In March of 2019, Charlie and Dana Stephenson purchased this historic property and began a meticulous restoration. Like the Snow family before them, the Stephensons believe that Waverley is treasure to be shared with the public. And the spirits of Waverley are content to remain and play an integral role in its ongoing story.

14

Cemeteries

I am not now
That which I have been.
—George Gordon Byron, *Childe Harold's Pilgrimage*

Cemeteries are where mortal bodies are buried. To soften the blow, the dead are spoken of in an array of euphemisms: *The dearly departed. The recently deceased. They have either passed, passed on, been laid to rest, gone to their final reward, met their maker, or moved on to a better place.* The collective dead are buried *six feet under*, or as one novice television reporter recently gushed, "waiting to be *funeralized.*" They have in more colloquial terms *kicked the bucket, croaked, or given up the ghost.*

Mississippi's cemeteries are a haven for haunted tales. The gravesites that fuel the stories range in size and scope. At McRaven House in Vicksburg, they are just depressions in the ground. Caretaker Leonard Fuller watches over them. "Outside this window here, you see a flat area, just past the oak tree. There are twenty-eight gravesites. McRaven House was used as a hospital during the Civil War, and a battle took place in the side yard near the railroad tracks where the Kansas City Southern goes by now. We've done some soundings. By the way they are buried, we know they are old military graves. We don't know who they are, but their ghosts still walk around here. The ghosts of Confederate soldiers have been seen since I was a kid."

In 2000, the current owner of McRaven, Leyland French, placed a simple gray stone plaque into the ground to mark the spot.

KNOWN BUT TO GOD
UNKNOWN CONFEDERATE DEAD
1863
LEST WE FORGET

A family graveyard is hidden in a tangle of fallen limbs and thick vines in West Point, Mississippi. The body of the little girl ghost who haunts Waverley Plantation is buried by the side of her grandfather, Dr. William Burt. Next to the Burts are the mortal remains of the Youngs, their neighbors in life and in death. The Youngs and the Burts both lost sons in battle during the Civil War. Descendants of the Youngs still return. They plant daffodils. They mourn the dead. And they worry.

Across the road at Waverley Plantation, Melanie Snow sighs, "Halloween is a big time here. People come and expect to see ghosts." Vandals covered the walls of Waverley in graffiti when it sat vacant for fifty years. The Burt and Young family plots have suffered an even greater indignity.

The Burt family plot across the road from Waverley Plantation.

The Burt vaults are set in the ground. Hooligans have shifted the heavy slab covers aside and have chipped away at the graves. On the Young side, a metal sign with white block letters is nailed to a filigreed iron fence surrounding the tombstones.

GEORGE HAMPTON
YOUNG
FAMILY CEMETERY
PLEASE RESPECT THE
RESTING PLACE OF OUR DEAD

Although the small cemetery is crowded, Melanie Snow believes there is room for one more grave. A nagging dream haunts her sleep. "Beverly Young was the only one of Colonel Young's sons to be wounded in battle. He died from infection and was buried up north. Forty-something of the Youngs are buried in that cemetery which used to be part of the Waverley Plantation property, all except Beverly. He haunts my dreams. I want to bring him home." Melanie Snow has even made plans. "He would come down this one-mile road in front of Waverley Plantation in a horse drawn carriage, and then he could finally be at peace with his family." Melanie is not sure if her persistent dream, inspired by the spirit of Beverly Young, will ever be a reality, but she is not giving up hope.

Burial records are problematic whether they sit on private property or state and federal lands. Names and dates are lost; tombs are vandalized or erode away from the effects of nature and time.

In Columbus, Mississippi, Nancy Carpenter, the project manager for the Columbus/Lowndes County Convention and Visitors Bureau, works feverishly to clear leaves and fallen branches from the pathways in the seventy acres of Friendship Cemetery. Volunteer students move into place for the twentieth anniversary of the dramatic rendering of Tales of the Crypt, the annual cemetery tour. Carpenter, an energetic woman with a wedge of blond hair and arresting blue eyes, warns that this is not a "pop-out-of-the-grave, I'm-going-to-get-you, blood-curdling affair." Tales of the Crypt was created by Carl Butler to help visitors see beyond the tombstones and learn how the deeds of the deceased continue to have impact.

On a bluff overlooking the Tombigbee River, the blossom-laden

The vandalized Young family tombs adjoin their neighbors.

branches of sun-dappled magnolia and dogwood trees shroud row upon row of small, anonymous headstones. The bloody battle of Shiloh delivered more than two thousand Confederate dead and a smattering of their foe to be buried here. Friendship Cemetery has a small town ambiance and a well-justified reputation as the cemetery where "Flowers Healed a Nation."

On April 25, 1866, a group of mothers and wives met at Twelve Gables, the home of the John Morton family. The women devised a plan to honor the Confederate soldiers newly interred in the cemetery. As the flowers were placed on the graves, one woman's heart broke. "I am a mother; I cannot put flowers on the Confederate graves and leave those of the Union boys barren." Carpenter quotes from this tearful episode. "And in a spontaneous moment all the other mothers joined her in showering flowers on the graves of all the young boys on both sides."

The Teasdale angel grieves for the dead in Friendship Cemetery.

This act of kindness in Friendship Cemetery sparked the American celebration of Memorial Day to honor fallen veterans no matter the battle, the war, or sides taken. Pale figures in uniform, restless spirits all, they are honored for their courage and sacrifice.

> *From the silence of sorrowful hours*
> *The desolate mourners go.*
> *Lovingly laden with flowers*
> *Alike for the friend and foe;*
> *Under the sod and the dew,*
> *Waiting the Judgment Day;*
> *Under the roses, the Blue*
> *Under the lilies, the Gray.*
> —F. M. Finch, "The Blue and the Gray"

Five young girls buried together at the Natchez City Cemetery did not die defending any cause. They simply went to work. On March 14, 1908, Carrie Murray, Ada White, Inez Netterville, Luella Booth, and Lizzie Worthy sat at a long, wooden table and poured chemicals from large beakers to smaller ones in the fourth-floor laboratory of the Natchez Drug Company. Carrie, the oldest, was twenty-two. Mary Elizabeth Worthy, "Lizzie," was one month short of her thirteenth birthday. At eleven o'clock in the morning, Sam Burns of the F. Mack Plumbing Company arrived to check on a recently installed gas heater. He detected a leak in the meter, tightened it up, and left. At 1:30 in the afternoon, Sam was called back. Someone still smelled gas. He rechecked the joints and junctions in the laboratory and found nothing. He headed downstairs to the first floor.

Sam did as he had been trained. He ran a lit candle along the gas line; if his candle flame flared, it would reveal the location of the gas leak. Sam found the leak. The explosion rocked the city and blew a hole twenty feet wide. Like a house of cards, the brick building imploded. The rear wall fell in, the east wall came down, and the upper floors collapsed all the way to the cellar. The flames spread out fueled by drugs, chemicals, oils, and other combustibles.

The body of seventeen-year-old Inez had been blown to the north part of the building near the sidewalk. Carrie was found in the rubble; rescue workers identified the body by her corset cover. Nineteen-year-old Ada's body had to be carried away in pieces. Luella's body was charred almost beyond recognition. She was nineteen. Workers didn't find Lizzie until three days later. They knew it was her because it was the smallest body recovered.

The girls' simple headstones are lined side by side. Over them looms the Natchez cemetery's signature statue, the "Turning Angel." She sits on a pedestal, a book open in her lap. Those who drive by Cemetery Road at night swear the white angel turns her head to look at them. As their cars pass the angel, she turns back to guarding her young charges, resting in their tombs beneath her. The effect is unsettling.

Eerier still is the Angels on the Bluff walking tour conducted in the weeks leading up to Halloween. Actors, portraying some of the cemetery's more notable citizens, take their place beside the tombs. On this night, a grieving father holds a lantern in his hand. "My name is Quinn Booth. They searched the rubble for three days before they found the charred remains of my daughter Luella. They buried her here with four others, and later the Natchez Drug Company raised this angel to look over the poor innocents." The tragic father figure laments, "They should have buried me at the same time." Quinn Booth never got over his daughter's death. For eight years, he stumbled about in a cloud of grief and depression. He blamed himself for insisting that his seventeen-year-old daughter get a job, no matter how menial. "It was my fault she was sitting at that table the day Sam Burns held a candle to check for gas leaks." Quinn Booth's grave is to the left and a few yards behind that of the girls. "It was the closest they could get me to my darling Luella."

It is an unseasonably warm October night in Natchez, the air stifling. Those gathered to hear Quinn Booth's tale clasp their arms around their chests to ward off a sudden chill. They make futile attempts to dispel the tingles creeping up and over their bodies. Tears flow as visitors bend to read the names etched into the headstones. A woman in her forties is rooted to a spot in front of young Lizzie's weathered grave. "She's staring at me. I can see her eyes. They are so sad. She still doesn't understand what happened." The woman in the navy-blue pantsuit appears as traumatized by her vision as the young victim in the grave at her feet.

The mysterious Turning Angel guards the graves of five young girls buried together in Natchez City Cemetery.

Other markers in this massive cemetery date back to the late 1700s. The graveyard is divided into plots like small neighborhoods, where the long-deceased residents still mix and mingle. In the Washington Ford lot, many believe that the mother of poor little Florence "Irene" Ford still tries to comfort her daughter. Certainly, this inconsolable parent went to extraordinary lengths to allay her daughter's fears.

Ten-year-old Irene died of yellow fever on October 30, 1871. She was terrified of storms and lightning. Ellen Ford had a concrete stairway built behind her daughter's headstone that led down to the level of the casket, where a glass window allowed her to look in. The child's casket also had a glass window on top. When it stormed, heedless of the rain pelting her head and shoulders, the protective mother climbed down the stairs. Ellen Ford was said to have talked, read, prayed, and sang to her daughter, trying to console her even in death. In later years, the grave became a popular draw to curiosity seekers. To keep the inquisitive out, cemetery workers erected a brick wall at the bottom of the stairwell and a hinged metal trap door to cover the opening. Oddly, Ellen Ford is not buried next to her daughter. There is no record of this devoted mother's final resting place. The Natchez City Cemetery is closed at night, but those who have made clandestine forays to little Irene's grave report sightings of the shape of a woman kneeling near the burial site. In *Legends of the Natchez City Cemetery,* author Don Estes describes an "eerie green glow" at the grave. The caretaker picked up a glowing orb from the site and showed it to his wife and daughter. But the orb dissipated when he opened his hands. Estes states that this incident in 1991 is the only corroborated ghost story at the cemetery.

Haunted tales also swirl about two other female graves in this legendary cemetery. One has sunk into the ground so far the inscription may soon be indecipherable. The mysterious headstone bears only a first name and a very strange two-word epitaph.

LOUISE
THE UNFORTUNATE

Louise was a prostitute who worked in Natchez-under-the-Hill, the city's notorious red-light district, which hugged a steep bank of the

Mississippi River. In the spring of 1849, she fell ill. Reverend Stratton, the local Presbyterian minister, offered assistance. Although she accepted his offer of food and medicine, the stubborn woman would only reveal her first name. When she died, the reverend raised money for her burial and erected a tombstone. Research conducted in 2005 by Don Estes, the former director of the Natchez City Cemetery, finally produced a surname—Leroy. Feisty Louise has a last name at last, yet no one seems in any hurry to claim her as their own and inscribe Leroy on the stone. If her troubled spirit could change anything, the first task on her list would likely be to erase her rather ignominious "Unfortunate" epitaph.

No one has reported hearing Rosalie Beekman speaking up for herself in the afterlife, but her dying words are the stuff of legends. Seven-year-old Rosalie was the only person killed in Natchez as a result of the Civil War. In September of 1862, the Union gunboat USS *Essex* shelled Natchez for three hours. The citizenry panicked. Rosalie's father, Aaron Beekman, tried to lead his daughters to safety. As they scurried up Silver Street, Rosalie's nine-year-old sister screamed, "Papa, Rosalie fell down." The harried father urged her to get up and run. She is said to have solemnly replied, "I can't, Papa. I'm killed."

Carved into the upper curve of her headstone are a cluster of roses. The center rose is a tightly closed bud, a symbol of life that will never open its fragrant petals and bloom. "Rosalie Beekman would have been my great-great-great-aunt. My mother's grandmother was Hattie Beekman." Caroline Guido, owner of Glenburnie in Natchez, lives with the residual effects of senseless tragedy every day. Jennie Merrill, the previous owner of Glenburnie, was shot down trying to escape from her murderer. Rosalie was shot while trying to keep up with her sister and her father. The loss of innocent Rosalie still resonates in Caroline's family. Rosalie's grave is a challenge to find. Visitors scramble through narrow winding paths hoping to connect with the spirited little girl.

Wherever there is a cemetery, it is hallowed, haunted ground. Each tomb that survives is like a chapter in an old, discarded book, its edges frayed, its binder broken, its pages wrinkled and yellowed. However, the story that lies within is more than myth and legend. It is the final place where a once-vibrant person left his imprint in the fertile lands of Mississippi. Their stories are there to be gathered and cherished.

A little cherub marks an infant grave in Columbus's Friendship Cemetery.

Lagniappe: In the rural regions of the Mississippi Delta, many head-stones have been lost to the ravages of time and weather. Fortunately, organizations such as the Mt. Zion Memorial Fund and its founder, Skip Henderson, stepped in to preserve the final resting places of legendary blues musicians such as Charley Patton. "Our work," says Henderson, "isn't some hollow gesture to honor the blues. . . . The Mt. Zion Memorial Fund serves as a legal conduit to provide financial and technical support for Black church communities and cemeteries in the Mississippi Delta."

Created in 2006, the Mississippi Blues Trail runs through the heart of the Delta and includes 210 (and counting) distinctive markers at sites such as cemeteries to recognize the impact on contemporary music by legends such as Charley Patton and Robert Johnson. Headstones and highway markers are merely the physical signposts, the reminders, that we are connected to a rich past that continues to shape who we are.

Epilogue

And life will be
as it has always been—
cycles within a circle,
whirling
without starts or finishes,
through the timeless places
of forever.
—Jim Metcalf, "Exodus"

If we see them only as shadows, wispy figures, or momentary aberrations, how do we know they are real? Why do we believe?

As a young teenager, Steven Johnson, president of the Robert Johnson Blues Foundation, was aware of the mythology and mystery surrounding his grandfather. Articles like those in the *New York Times* and accounts by the National Park Service contributed to the rumors that Robert Johnson, the "King of the Delta Blues," can't find eternal rest. Given the fact that grave markers have been erected at three different Greenwood-area sites, it is understandable that Johnson's spirit is a bit confused and wanders about.

Personal experiences can transform nonbelievers into believers. Kathy Hall had never given much thought to the ability of the dead to return until she was twenty-one. "I was three-months pregnant with my first child when my husband passed away. I never expected to have such a drastic thing happen to me. It was hard for me to get a grip on reality. After several months of trying to deal with the idea of his death, I sat out in my front yard one night and I just looked up at the sky and I said, 'I can't do this. You've got to help me through this.'" Hall takes a deep breath. "It was like he put his hand on my shoulder. I could feel it. So yeah, I believe they can come back. I believe they do come back."

Before she came to work the front desk at Cedar Grove Inn in Vicksburg, Hall had never heard the stories about its ghosts. Seven years into the job, she has met most of them. "I have seen the little handprints on the wall in the Bonnie Blue room. I have smelled the cigar smoke in the gentlemen's parlor before the guests arrive. I have seen the photographs."

Hall was present on one occasion when the ghosts had their pictures taken. "I took a couple on a tour one morning. The husband took pictures inside and outside of the library suite, room 21. Afterwards, he loaded the pictures in his laptop and showed them to me. One was in the sitting room; you could see the settee and over it the gold frame of the painting with birds in it, except in the photo the birds were gone. There was just a white blur blocking them. I jokingly said, 'Well, Mr. Klein was in here with y'all.' I guess he stepped into the frame just when they snapped the picture."

In a second photo, there is a close-up of the oval plaque on the door to the suite. "There were these fire flames shooting up. Really cool," declares Hall. The front desk manager's explanation of the paranormal evidence is that the flames were from Mr. Klein's cigar as his spirit was about to enter his favorite room. "Each one of us who have been at Cedar Grove Inn for a while, John, Joe, myself, we all respect this house and we respect the ghosts."

Joe Connor, the head bartender, says that occasionally things get a little too real for some staff members. "We had a waitress, Christina, who had been here off and on for a couple of years. During Halloween, she'd get dressed up as Mrs. Elizabeth Klein, the former lady of Cedar Grove. The last time, last October, in the middle of the tour, she got out of her costume and quit. She said the ghosts were messing with her; she could hear them whispering, 'We're back.' She just ran off, that's how spooked she was."

Chef John Kellogg feels the ghosts are usually a bit more subtle. "Joe will be standing at the bar and you'll see him do this." Kellogg takes his hand and flicks at the back of his neck as if trying to shoo something or someone away. "We put Ashley, one of our new girls, behind the bar one night to train, and she said, 'I don't know what it is. Something keeps tugging at my hair or pulling at my shirt collar.'" The executive chef offers reassurance. "It is never anything scary. It happens so often that we don't even pay attention to it anymore. It's nothing major."

Dixie Butler, the owner of Temple Heights in Columbus, is philosophical on the subject of ghosts. "There are a lot of things you just can't explain; our minds are so finite we can't conceive of what it could be."

Kay McNeil lived and worked at Magnolia Hall in Natchez. She regrets that she never reached a more personal level with Mr. Henderson whose spirit roams the house. "I don't know if you have to be in a special mode or a special person for him to want to talk to you. Many times I would sit in the hallway right by the room where he died, or I would play the piano with my back to his bedroom, hoping he would talk to me. I felt him there, but he would never say anything. I still get goose bumps. Maybe I just wasn't the right person, so I guess he is still waiting to get his message across."

Tom Miller, the proprietor of King's Tavern in Natchez thinks it's a seasonal thing. "Since it has turned warm, we usually go through some stale periods where not much happens in the way of haunting. Nobody reports seeing our ghost girl Madeline. We get very little paranormal activity in the summer." Miller shrugs. "I don't know why, maybe the ghosts head up north where it's cool." Miller is not worried. He's confident alluring Madeline will be back come fall.

Historian and cultural anthropologist, Dr. Elizabeth Boggess doesn't believe it has anything to do with the weather or any earthly outside influences. For Boggess, spirits tend to behave in the same manner that they did when they were alive. "My husband died in a plane crash. Right after his death and before he was buried, they were about to bring the body home, and I had gone to my mother's house because I couldn't be left alone. I woke up from a nap, and I knew that my husband was on one side of the bed and his best friend, who was killed with him, was on the other side. I am convinced that a spirit comes back because they may have something else to do." Boggess is a practical woman resigned to the inevitable. "After the funeral, I never had any sense that my husband was there, but his best friend was. He was a born wanderer, and I think he just had a need to keep wandering."

Jeanette Feltus runs Linden solo. When her husband was alive, he assisted with the operation of the popular bed and breakfast on the outskirts of Natchez. "I would fuss at Richard because he would spread paperwork all over the kitchen." Feltus had an office built for her husband's exclusive use over the garage. "He didn't like being so far removed from what was going on here, so he'd dump his stuff back on the kitchen table." She looks over her kitchen with a sly grin. An answering machine, a copier, a fax machine, brochures, and reservation forms are stacked up on every level. "I can hear Richard laughing whenever I am in here because the kitchen is where I run the business now." Feltus embraces all of her family ghosts and informs overnight guests that while Linden is definitely haunted, all of the spirits, including her late husband, are quite friendly.

"Of course," nods a sage Tom Miller, "nobody wants to scare anybody off telling them there are evil spirits. Each of the homes I owned here in Natchez had an entity in it, different kinds. People ask me if I'm scared, if they keep me up at night." Miller sits in the bar he owns along with King's Tavern, the adjacent haunted restaurant. "I'm used to it. I don't think we have evil entities here, but we had an investigative team here once and they recorded this demonic voice." Miller boots up his computer and plays the recording. A deep voice intones, *'I'm here on the porch.'* Miller closes the laptop and polishes off his drink. "Yeah, it does alarm me a little bit."

Patricia Taylor runs into ghosts no matter where she goes. During the annual Spring Pilgrimage in Natchez, she puts up with the antics of Thomas Henderson's spirit at Magnolia Hall. When she's on a break from docent duties, apparitions like to check her out. "There is a courtyard at the Eola Hotel where on a nice day you can sit outside and eat lunch. I was there with a friend, and I could see this gentleman standing in the corner. He didn't move, and I asked my friend if she knew the man because he kept staring at us. She said, 'There is nobody there, Patricia.'" Taylor allows that she tends to be "a bit sensitive" to the paranormal. This time she decided the ghost should acknowledge her. "I walked past him, and I sort of nodded, and he nodded back at me." Taylor would love to know the identity of the courtyard ghost. "The man was there for a reason. There's got to be a picture of him in this town somewhere; he was wearing a frock coat when I realized it."

With Taylor, spectral encounters are like tag teams; one hooks on to another. "I talked to the manager of the Eola, and she found my experience quite interesting. She took my friend and I into one of the rooms she believes is exceptionally haunted. She and her family used the room when they first moved to Natchez. They had to move out because she said all four of them heard strange noises, not normal hotel noises." Taylor felt very ill at ease in the room. She discovered that the hotel has an untold quantity of what she refers to as "residual memories." The staff speaks of literally running into the ghost of Isadore Levy, who built the hotel in 1927, and his daughter, Eola, for whom the hotel was named. Eola died at sixteen, and her spirit often gives guests a little nudge on the staircase. Patricia Taylor would have preferred bumping into Eola rather than what she saw as she tried to ascend the staircase.

"Bodies wrapped in shrouds, in rows, about yeah far off the floor," Taylor raises her arm waist high. "I couldn't walk upstairs because that meant I would have to walk through them. I have tried and tried to find out what went on there. It was not a Confederate hospital; it was built in the early 1920s I think." Taylor did a little research and arrived at a more likely scenario for her vision at the hotel. "Someone told me that there was a hurricane that came through here in the early 1800s and it killed a lot of people. They would have had to store them somewhere, so maybe before this was a hotel, there was an open space that they used as a triage center of some sort."

Judy Grimsley served as head docent at Magnolia Hall in Natchez for many years. She argues on the side of ghosts. "To me, hauntings are just like déjà vu. Those feelings you get like you were there before. You already know what someone is going to say. No one can explain that. Why is it so hard to believe that there are ghosts?"

Kathleen Blankenstein, who has served on the board governing nearby Magnolia Hall, is puzzled. "Why do people want to believe—just because it's fun?" Although she is firmly in the doubter's camp, this longtime resident of Natchez does try to keep an open mind—until proven otherwise. On an outing to the Natchez City Cemetery, she met with Donald Estes, the cemetery director. "Don was telling me he thought there was a body here at this place where we were getting ready to put a tombstone to this Spanish American soldier. He said he was pretty sure, but he would use his equipment to confirm it." Blankenstein visibly winces. "He believes in dousing. He had these two coat hangers and he held them like this." Blankenstein crosses her arms. "He passed these hangers over the ground and told me if they bent one way it meant something and if they went the other way it meant something else. I was just laughing, but he was quite serious. He said, 'It will not only tell you if there is a body there, it will tell you whether it was male or female.'"

Blankenstein backtracks in her story and gives a brief run down of some family names. "We had a Josephine, a Lily, and a Shirley. My father's given name was Shirley. He was named for a friend who's surname was Shirley. Now most people think of it as a girl's name. My father said he never had a fight over it until Shirley Temple came along."

A doubtful Blankenstein watched as Estes demonstrated his dousing method. "He held the dousing hangers over Josephine's grave without looking down and said, 'It's a female.' He came to Lily, did the same thing and said it was another female," Blankenstein can barely contain a wide grin. "He got to my father's grave and said, 'That's a female.' And I shouted, 'Gottcha!' Don leaned over to read the name and he couldn't understand. He said, 'Let me see. That says Shirley, so that's a female.' I said, 'Don, that's my father, and he's not a female.'" Blankenstein's good-natured laugh erupts. She composes herself and tries for a bit more understanding of people's fascination with all things paranormal. "Maybe there is something to it. It's just not for me."

Nancy Carpenter is on the same page. "I personally don't believe in ghosts, but I love a good story."

Grayce Hicks of Rosewood Manor in Columbus isn't sure how the stories got started at her historic Greek Revival mansion. Over the years, the home has been known by many names—Birdhaven, Wooten Manor, Fairleigh Manor, Maydrew Manor—before settling into Rosewood Manor. The cavernous home was built in 1835 by Richard Skyes as a townhouse to entertain his many acquaintances. "This house has a complete basement, almost an entire other house underneath where the servants' quarters were." Grayce and her husband, Dewitt Hicks, use the space now for storage, but aspects of its past can't be erased. "Some people are scared to death of our basement. They think it is haunted."

On a beautiful spring day, gardeners are busy sprucing up the grounds.

There are more than 4.5 acres of gardens, three thousand boxwoods, a rose garden, and an herb garden in this floral fantasyland. Hicks observes one of the maintenance men skirt the basement door. "They think there are ghosts in there." Hicks finds the notion nearly incomprehensible. "I have lived here for thirty-three years and haven't met a ghost yet." With her distinct Southern inflection, she states with no hesitation, "I don't feel like I am missing anything because I might be scared if I was. This is a large house and you know, as they say . . . *if walls could talk.*"

Mattie Jo Ratcliffe, the former chairwoman of the Natchez Pilgrimage Club, also has definite opinions. "I know there is an element out there that we don't understand and we don't know about. And in my opinion, a house, a home, a building that's been sitting there since the 1800s that has witnessed laughter and tears and emotions of all kinds . . . why wouldn't it absorb some of those feelings, some of those emotions?" She answers her own question. "I think having ghost stories is good. I do. When my husband and I bought a historic home, it was a tremendous redo. There was a threshold in the back of the hall that originally had been the back gallery. The threshold was a worn-away, wide cypress log. I told my husband that I would just love to know how many feet had crossed that log and who they belonged to. I think when you personalize history, it makes it alive. That's what ghost stories do; you get to meet the people before you."

Appendix

For more information about the sites visited in this book, refer to the following list. The entries are grouped here by geographic region north to south.

HILLS REGION

Rowan Oak
719 Old Taylor Road
Oxford, MS 38655
662-234-3284

Saint Peter's Cemetery
Jefferson Avenue and North
   Sixteenth Street
Oxford, MS 38655

**Oxford Convention and Visitors
   Bureau**
102 Ed Perry Boulevard
Oxford, MS 38655
800-758-9177

**Elvis Presley Birthplace and
   Museum**
306 Elvis Presley Drive
Tupelo, MS 38801
662-841-1245

**Lyric-Tupelo Community
   Theatre**
200 North Broad Street
Tupelo, MS 38802
662-844-1935

**Tupelo Convention and Visitors
   Bureau**
399 East Main Street
Tupelo, MS
800-533-0611

DELTA REGION

**Greenville-Washington County
CVB (The Old Armory)**
216 South Walnut Street
Greenville, MS 38701
800-467-3582

**Greenville Iron Works (Artist
John Puddin' Moore)**
214 South Walnut Street
Greenville, MS 38701
662-332-8266

Delta Democrat Times **(original
building)**
Corner of Walnut and Main
Street
Greenville, MS 38701

Delta Democrat Times **(office)**
988 North Broadway
Greenville, MS 38701
662-335-1155

**Delta Center Stage Community
Theatre**
E. E. Bass Cultural Arts Center
323 South Main Street
Greenville, MS 38701
662-332-2246

Mt. Holly Plantation
(private)
Susie B. Law House
(private)

**Evergreen Cemetery and St.
John's Ruins**
East Lake Washington Road
Glen Allan, MS 38744

Southern Star/Bait-n-Thangs
1940 Lake Washington Road
Chatham, MS 38731
662-827-2666

**The Birthplace of the Frog: An
Exhibit of Jim Henson's
Delta Boyhood**
415 South Deer Creek Drive East
Leland, MS 38756
662-686-7383

PINES REGION

Waverley Mansion
1852 Waverley Mansion Road
West Point, MS 39773
662-494-1399

Rosedale
1523 Ninth Street South
Columbus, MS 39701
800-920-3533

Rosewood Manor
719 Seventh Street North
Columbus, MS 39701
662-328-7313

Temple Heights
515 Ninth Street North
Columbus, MS 39701
800-920-3533

Friendship Cemetery
Fourth Street South
Columbus, MS 39701
662-328-2569

**Tennessee Williams Welcome
Center**
**Columbus Spring Pilgrimage:
Tales from the Crypt and
Ghosts & Legends Tour**
300 Main Street
Columbus, MS 39701
800-920-3553

CAPITAL/RIVER REGION

The Old State Capitol Museum
100 South State Street
Jackson, MS 39205
601-576-6920

The Chapel of the Cross
674 Mannsdale Road
Madison, MS 39110
601-856-2953

Natchez City Cemetery
2 Cemetery Road
Natchez, MS 39120
601-445-5051

(Author photo courtesy of Jeffery D. Meyers)